NON VERBAL
TEST 9

Read the following instructions carefully:

1. Do not open this question booklet until you are instructed to do so.

2. This test has four sections, each containing 18 questions. There are 72 questions in total.

3. All your answers must be marked on the separate multiple choice sheet. Answers written on this question booklet will not be counted.

4. You may write any rough working on this question booklet.

5. For all questions you must select only one answer.

6. To mark your answer, draw a horizontal line through the rectangle next to your answer on the multiple choice sheet. If you want to change your answer, rub it out as completely as you can and then select your new answer.

7. Make sure you do not lose your place on the multiple choice sheet. Check that your answer box has the same number as the question that you are on.

8. You may not get to the end of the paper, but complete as many questions as you can. If a question is taking you too long, make sure you do not waste time on it and move forward to the next question. If you cannot decide which is the correct answer, select the one you think is most likely to be correct.

9. You have 50 minutes to complete this test. Work as quickly and carefully as you can.

Authors: Steven Vu and Graham Wildash

Published by Test Teach Limited.
Unit 203 Kingspark Business Centre, 152-178 Kingston Road, Kingston Upon Thames, KT3 3ST.

Test Teach

DO NOT OPEN THIS BOOKLET UNTIL TOLD TO DO SO

TYPE 2

In each question below, there are five shapes.

Find the shape that has the **least in common** with the four other shapes and mark its letter on the multiple choice sheet.

EXAMPLE 1 EXPLANATION

1. All of the choices contain a large white triangle which is pointing to the right, except **d**.

2. The answer, therefore, must be **d** as it doesn't have a characteristic that the other four choices share.

EXAMPLE 1

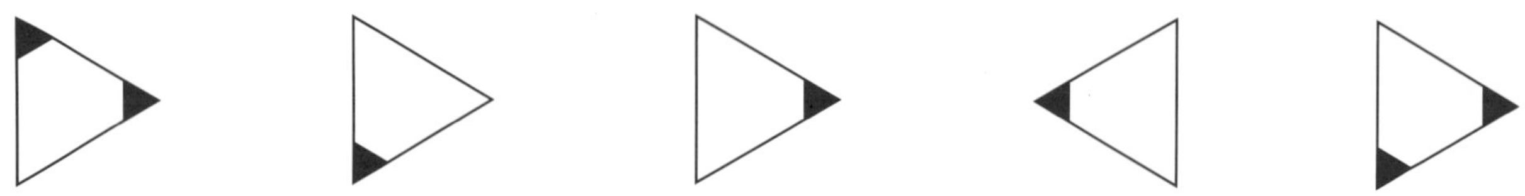

a b c d e

EXAMPLE 2

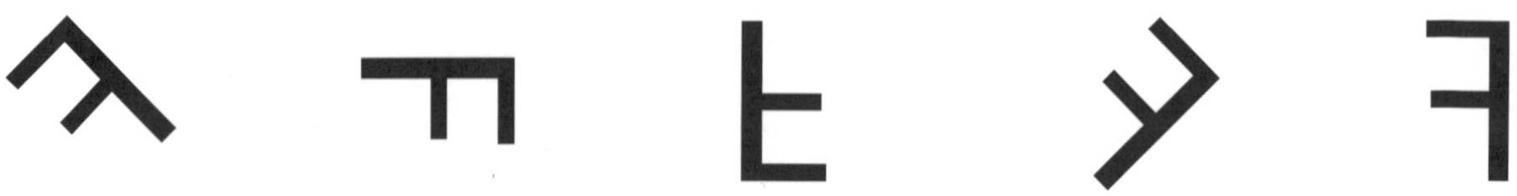

a b c d e

START OF SECTION

1

a b c d e

2

a b c d e

3

a b c d e

4

a b c d e

5

a b c d e

6

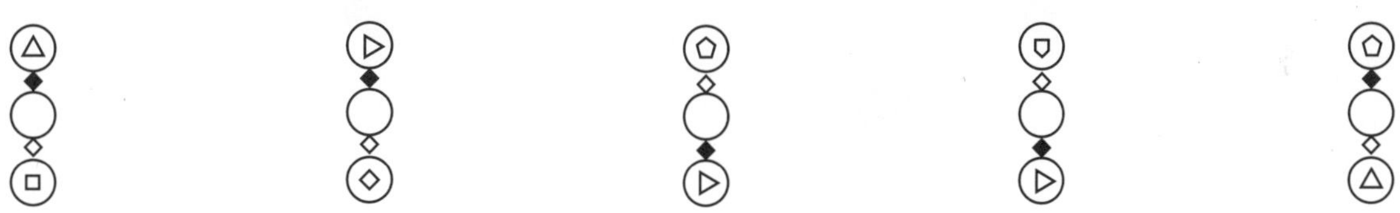

a b c d e

7

a b c d e

8

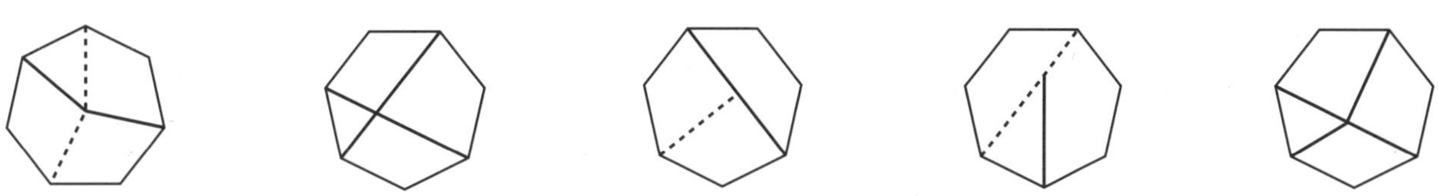

a b c d e

9

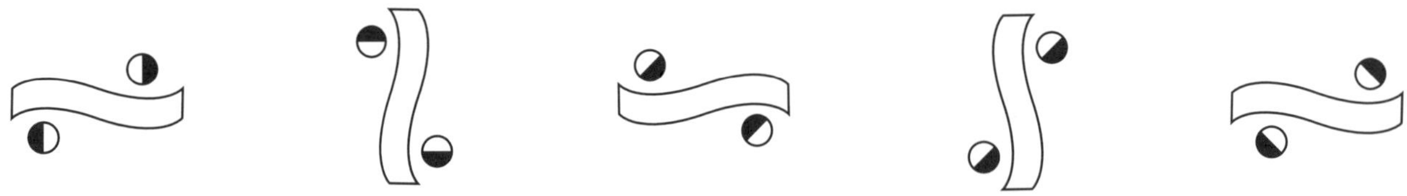

a b c d e

10

a b c d e

11

a b c d e

12

a b c d e

13

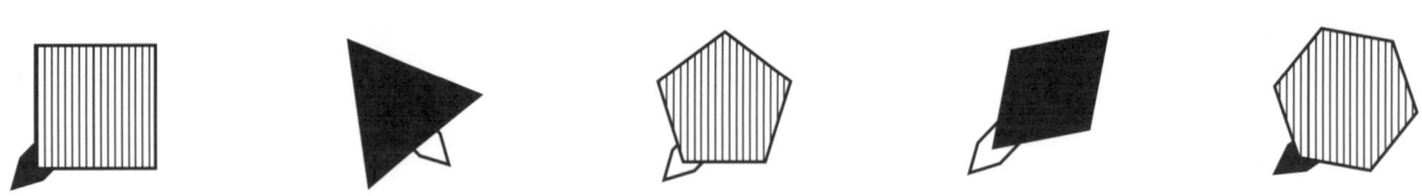

a b c d e

14

a b c d e

15

a b c d e

16

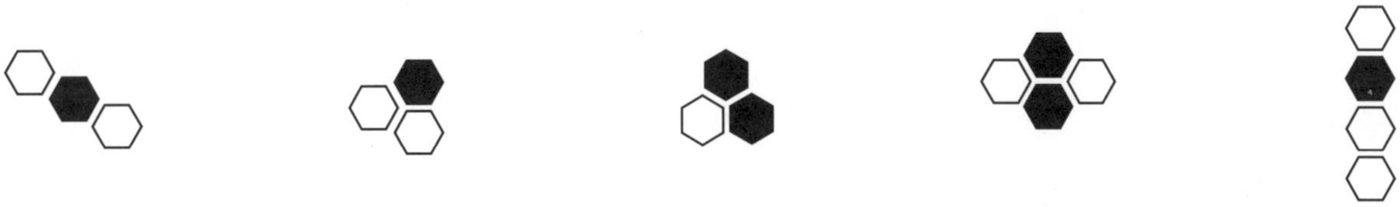

a b c d e

17

a b c d e

18

a b c d e

END OF SECTION

TYPE 5

In each question below, the shapes on the left have been identified with a code. Each letter in the code represents a **different characteristic** of the shapes.

By working out what the letters mean, you must select the correct code to **describe the new shape** you have been given.

Select the correct code from the five options on the right and mark its letter on the multiple choice sheet.

EXAMPLE 1 EXPLANATION

1. The first and last figure are the same shape and share the same first letter. The first letter, therefore, represents the shape of the figure so the first letter for our figure is D.

2. The first shape and the third shape are black and share the same second letter, therefore, the second letter represents shading. Our shape has the same shading as the second shape, so its second letter must be S.

EXAMPLE 1

DR
ES
GR
DG

ER	EG	GG	DS	GS
a	b	c	d	e

EXAMPLE 2

EDW
GSR
ESW
BDR

GDW	BSR	GDR	BSW	EDR
a	b	c	d	e

START OF SECTION

19

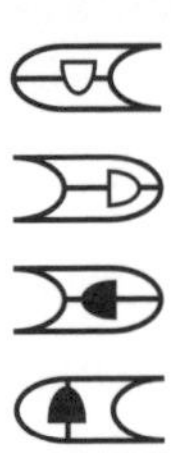

PYA
RZA
RXB
PVB

RYB	PXA	PVB	PZB	PVA
a	b	c	d	e

20

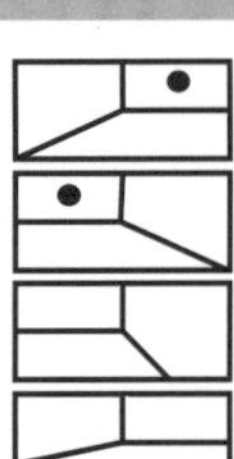

LOP
LYP
NYT
NOV

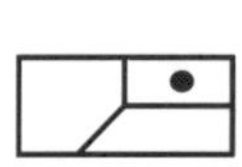

LYV	LOT	LOV	NOT	NOV
a	b	c	d	e

21

ZAP
XAL
YBK
VBL

YAK	ZBP	XBP	XAL	VAP
a	b	c	d	e

22

AJX
BJY
CKZ
DKY

DJZ	DKX	DJY	DKY	BJY
a	b	c	d	e

23

ZAT
YBS
ZCR
ZCS

YCR	YCS	YBR	ZBR	ZCT
a	b	c	d	e

24

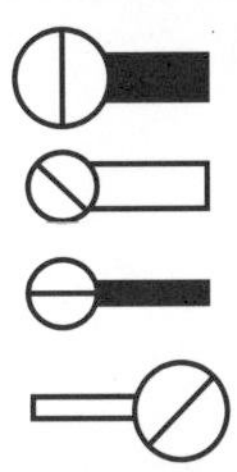

BGT
CGR
CHS
BHP

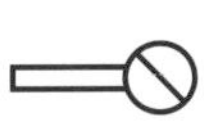

CHP	CGS	CHR	BHR	BGS
a	b	c	d	e

25

AZ
BY
CY
DX

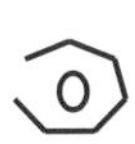

AY	BY	BZ	DZ	DY
a	b	c	d	e

26

HT
LP
HR
LY

HP	HY	HR	LP	LY
a	b	c	d	e

27

ATY
AHY
BTY
BHX

a	b	c	d	e
ATX	AHX	AHY	BHY	BTX

28

SWE
IRE
SVA
DRA

a	b	c	d	e
SRA	DWA	DVE	IWA	IVE

29

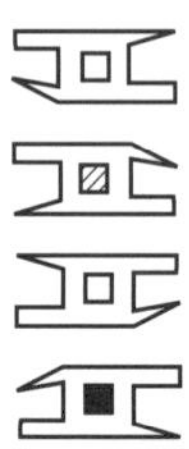

ZA
YB
XA
VC

a	b	c	d	e
VA	ZB	XB	XC	YC

30

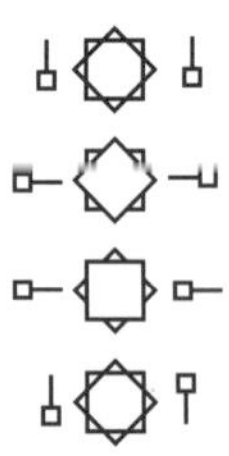

KI
BG
VI
KG

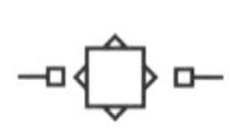

a	b	c	d	e
BI	BG	VG	VI	KI

31

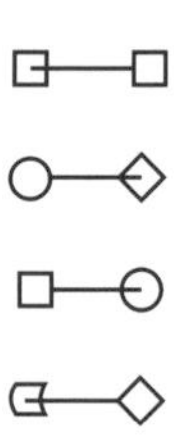

AP
EH
IP
BW

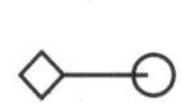

a	b	c	d	e
IH	BH	EP	IW	AW

32

AZ
BY
CZ
BX

a	b	c	d	e
BZ	BX	AY	AX	CZ

33

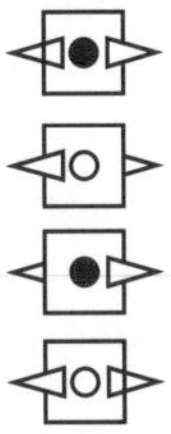

AZT
BYS
AZR
CYS

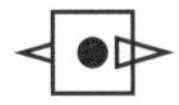

a	b	c	d	e
AYR	CYR	CZR	BZS	BYT

34

BYL
BYI
BXL
AZI

a	b	c	d	e
AXL	AZL	AXI	BZI	BZL

35

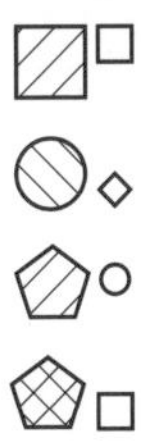

ACH
RGE
RCP
RVE

a	b	c	d	e
RCE	ACP	AVE	AVP	ACE

36

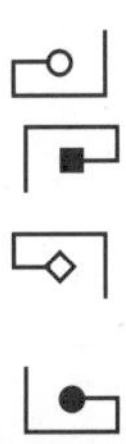

PAY
HBX
RCY
PDX

a	b	c	d	e
HCY	RBX	PDY	RCX	HDY

END OF SECTION

TYPE 3

In each question below, there are two shapes on the left hand side which are **related to each other**. To the right of the dots there is a third shape.

Pick a fourth shape from the five available options so that the third and fourth shape **share the same relationship** as the first and second shape.

Mark your choice on the multiple choice sheet.

EXAMPLE 1 EXPLANATION

1. In the first pair of shapes, the colour changes from white to black. Therefore, the shading of our shape, which is a white hexagon, must also change to black.

2. In the first pair of shapes, the first shape rotates 45° to give the second shape. Therefore, our shape must also rotate 45°.

3. In the first pair of shapes, the size of the first shape shrinks, therefore, our shape must become smaller.

EXAMPLE 1

a b c d e

EXAMPLE 2

a b c d e

START OF SECTION

37

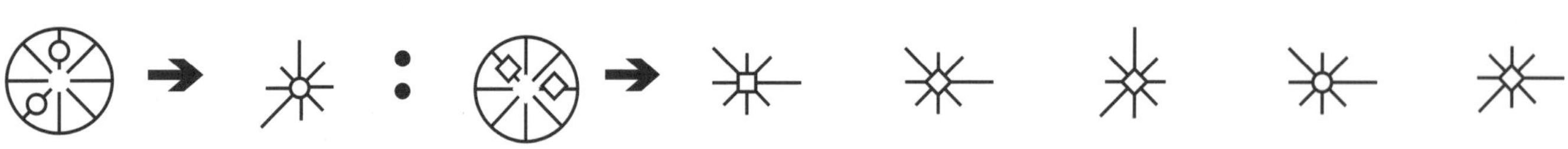

a b c d e

38

a b c d e

39

a b c d e

40

a b c d e

41

a b c d e

42

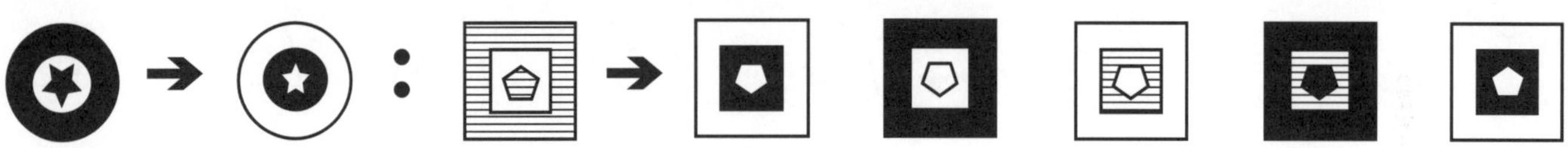

a b c d e

43

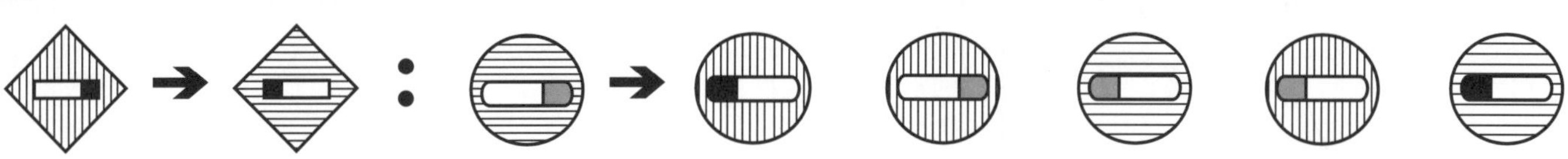

a b c d e

44

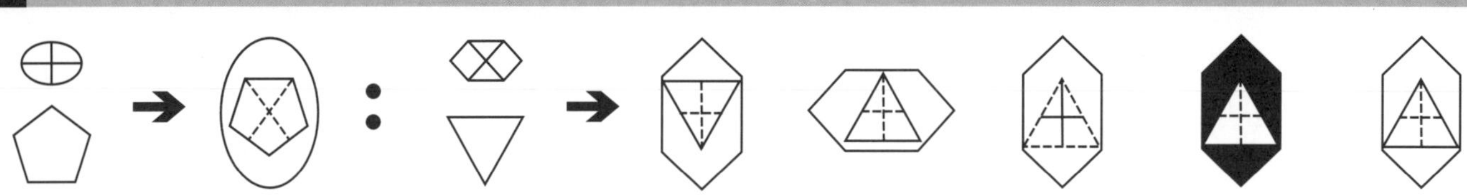

a b c d e

45

a b c d e

46

a b c d e

47

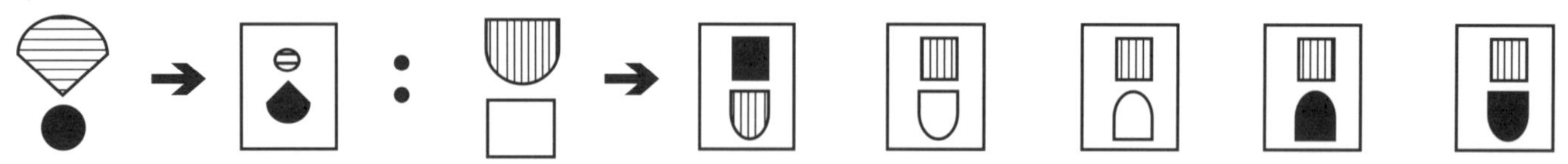

a b c d e

48

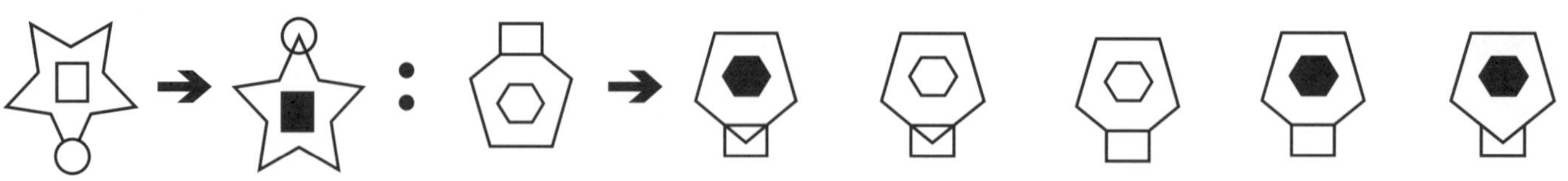

a b c d e

49

a b c d e

50

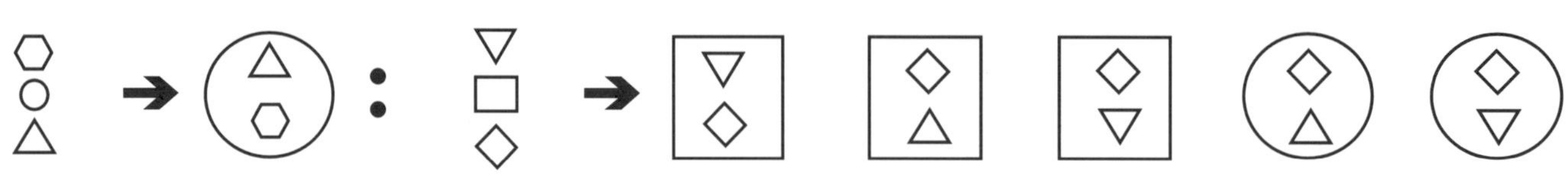

a b c d e

51

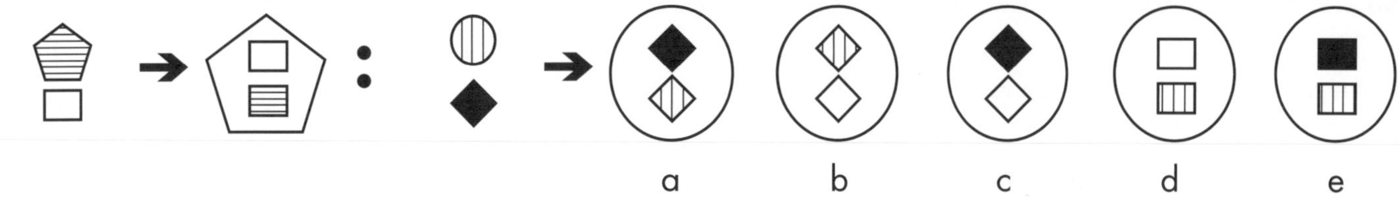

52

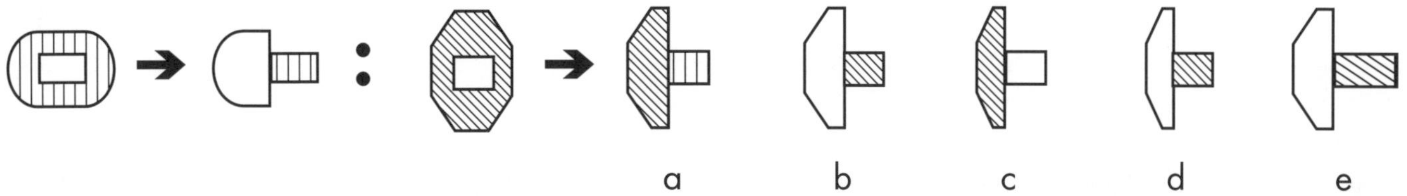

53

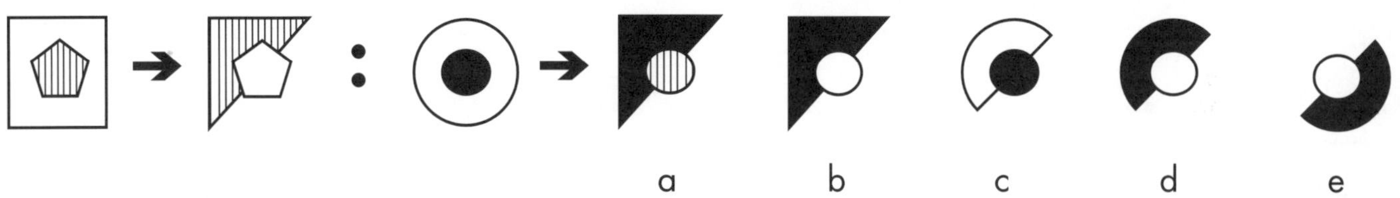

54

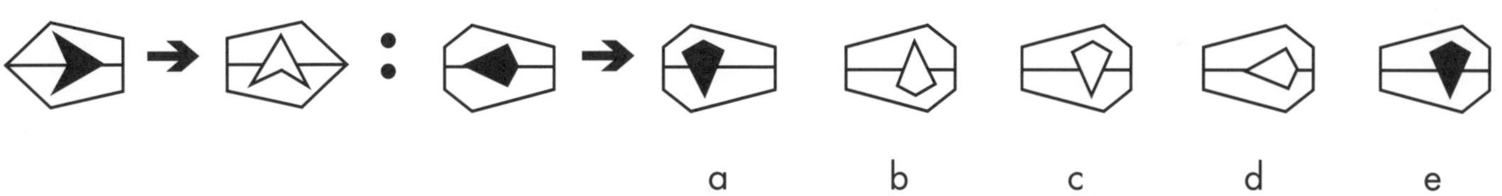

END OF SECTION

TYPE 7

In each question, five boxes have been **arranged in a sequence**. One box has been removed so that the sequence is no longer complete.

From the five options on the right, **find which box has been removed** and mark its letter on your multiple choice sheet.

EXAMPLE 1 EXPLANATION

1. The central shape is alternating in colour and shape. Our missing box, therefore, must contain a central shape which is a black square.

2. There is a small black square located in one of the corners in each box. It moves clockwise from corner to corner. Therefore, our missing box must also contain a small black square in its top left corner.

EXAMPLE 1

a b c d e

EXAMPLE 2

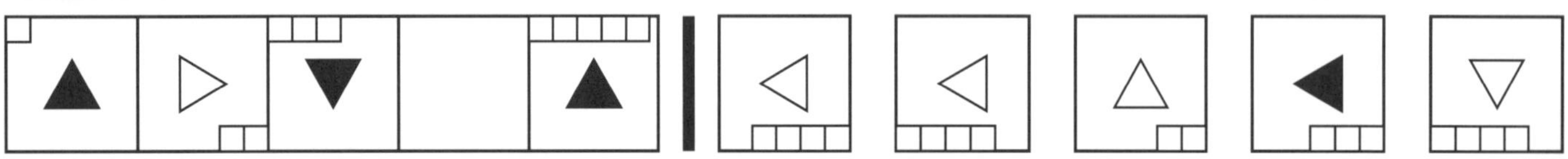

a b c d e

START OF SECTION

55

a b c d e

56

a b c d e

57

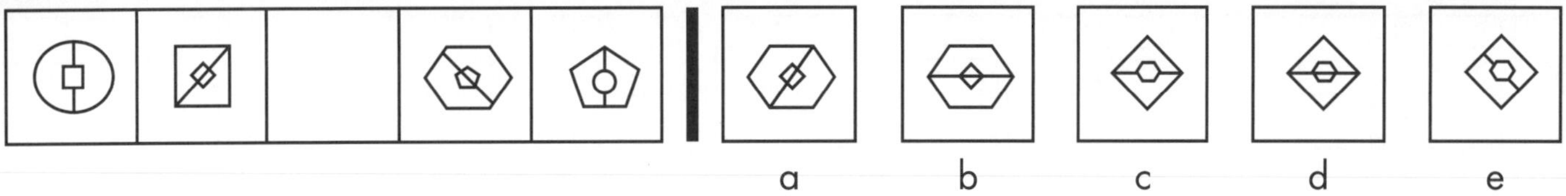

58

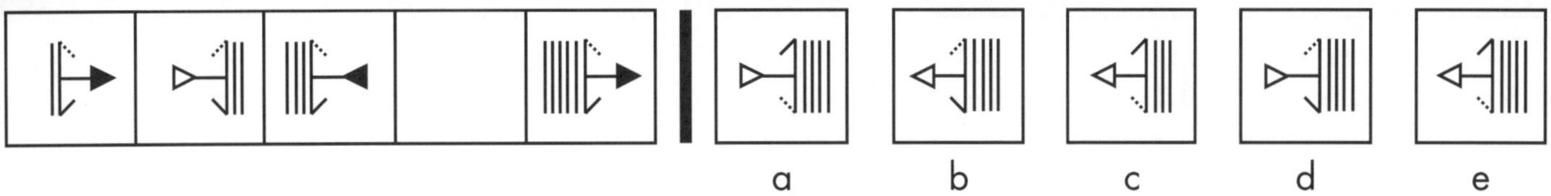

59

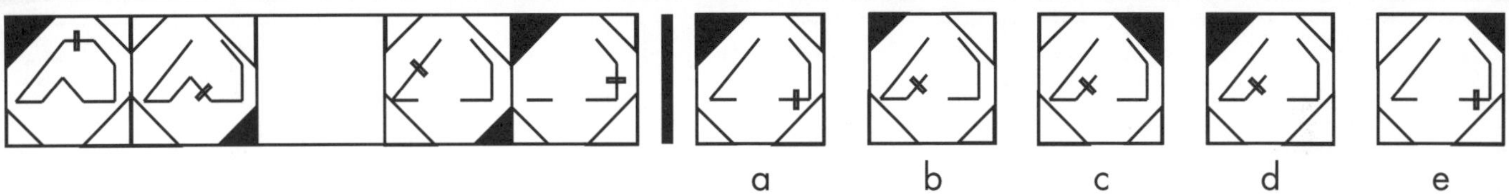

60

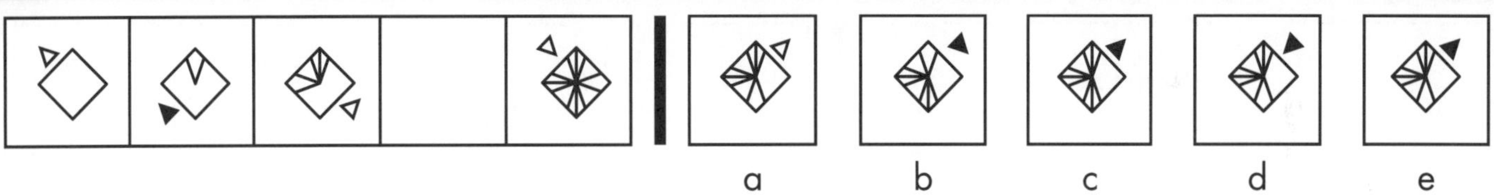

61

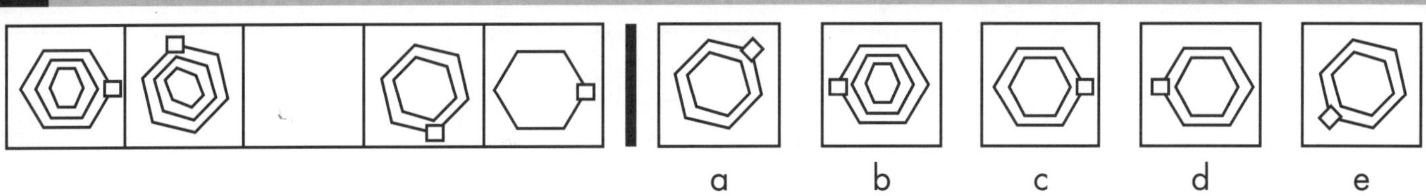

62

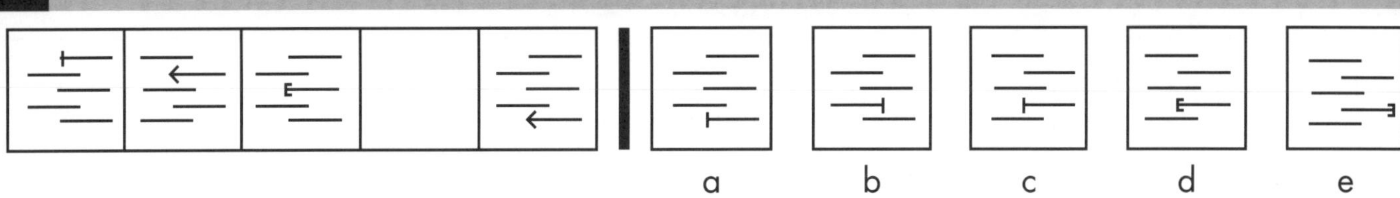

63

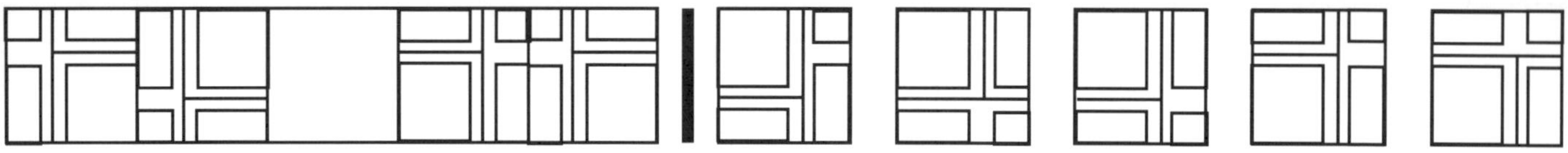

a b c d e

64

a b c d e

65

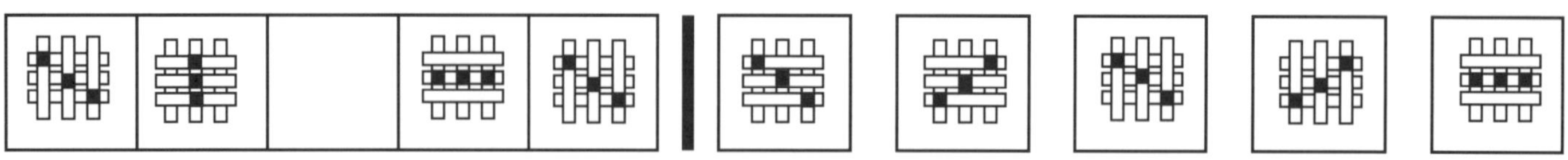

a b c d e

66

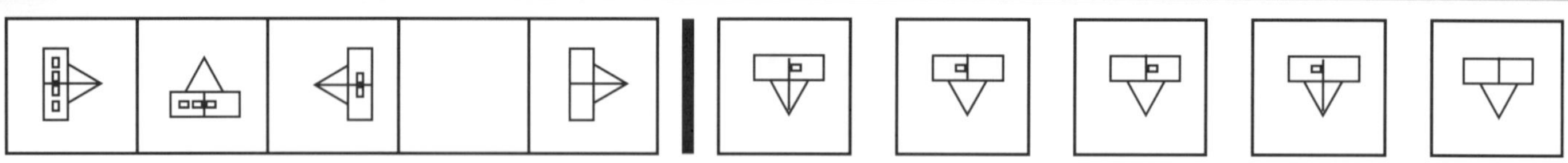

a b c d e

67

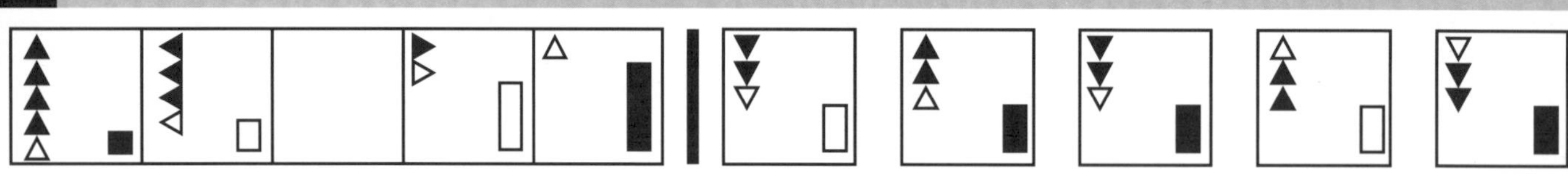

a b c d e

68

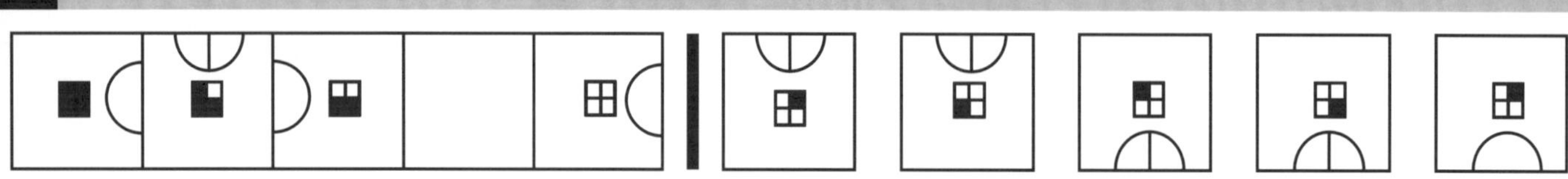

a b c d e

69

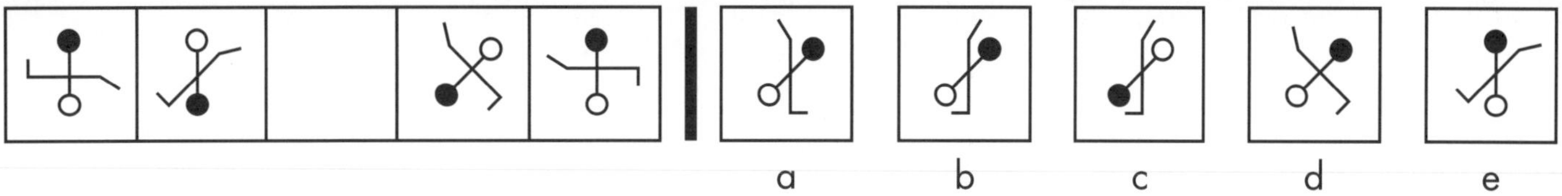

70

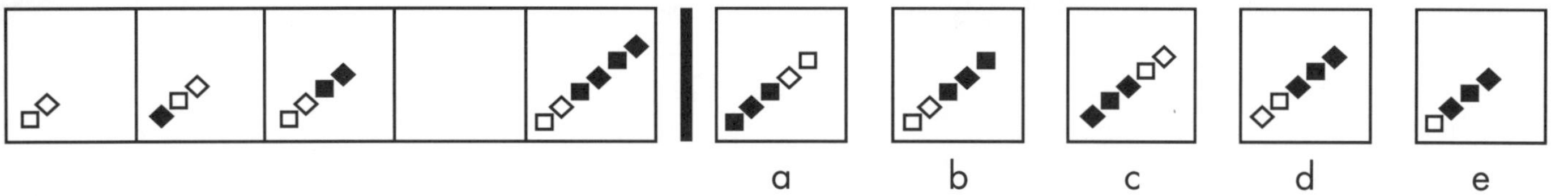

71

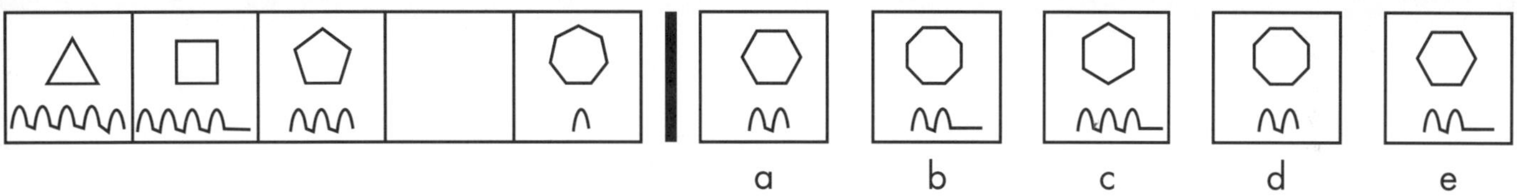

72

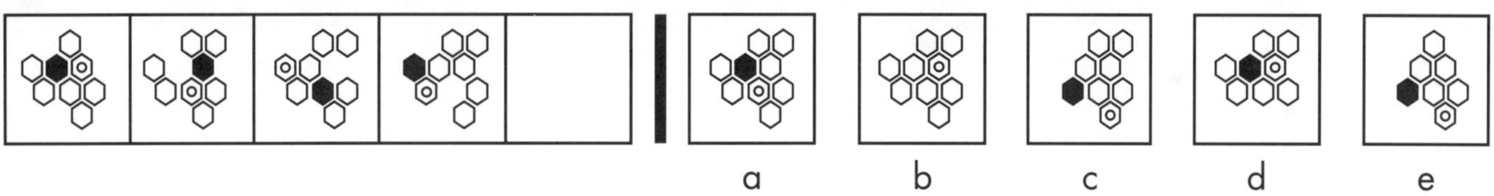

END OF TEST

[THIS PAGE IS INTENTIONALLY LEFT BLANK]

[THIS PAGE IS INTENTIONALLY LEFT BLANK]

NON VERBAL
TEST 10

Read the following instructions carefully:

1. Do not open this question booklet until you are instructed to do so.
2. This test has four sections, each containing 18 questions. There are 72 questions in total.
3. All your answers must be marked on the separate multiple choice sheet. Answers written on this question booklet will not be counted.
4. You may write any rough working on this question booklet.
5. For all questions you must select only one answer.
6. To mark your answer, draw a horizontal line through the rectangle next to your answer on the multiple choice sheet. If you want to change your answer, rub it out as completely as you can and then select your new answer.
7. Make sure you do not lose your place on the multiple choice sheet. Check that your answer box has the same number as the question that you are on.
8. You may not get to the end of the paper, but complete as many questions as you can. If a question is taking you too long, make sure you do not waste time on it and move forward to the next question. If you cannot decide which is the correct answer, select the one you think is most likely to be correct.
9. You have 50 minutes to complete this test. Work as quickly and carefully as you can.

Authors: Steven Vu and Graham Wildash

Published by Test Teach Limited.
Unit 203 Kingspark Business Centre, 152-178 Kingston Road, Kingston Upon Thames, KT3 3ST.

Test Teach

DO NOT OPEN THIS BOOKLET UNTIL TOLD TO DO SO

TYPE 1

In each question below, there is a grid which contains **one empty square**.

Determine which figure is missing from the empty square and mark its letter on your multiple choice sheet.

EXAMPLE 1 EXPLANATION

1. Each row contains figures of the same colour and shape. The missing square is in the top row and, therefore, must contain a black triangle.

2. Each column contains shapes of the same size. The missing square must, therefore, contain a large shape.

3. Having determined the logic that governs the rows and columns, we can now deduce that our shape must be a large black triangle.

EXAMPLE 1

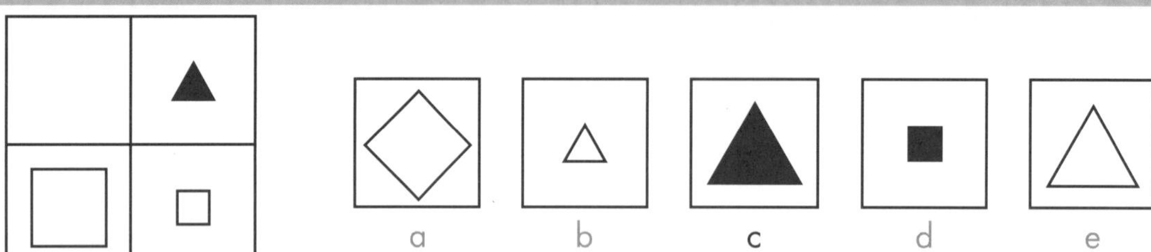

EXAMPLE 2

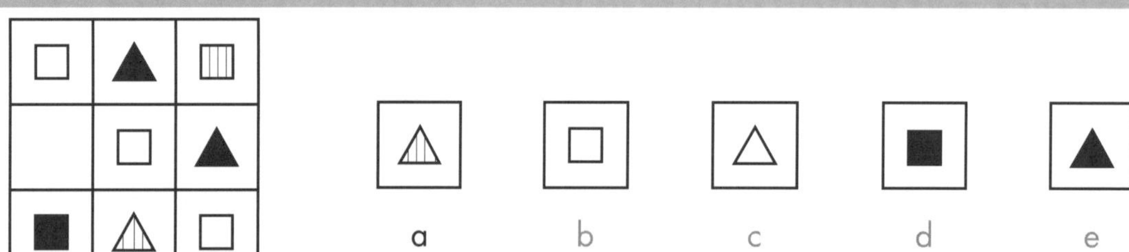

START OF SECTION

1

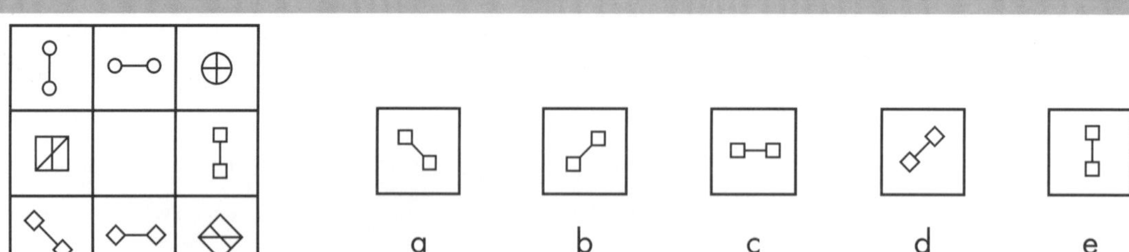

2

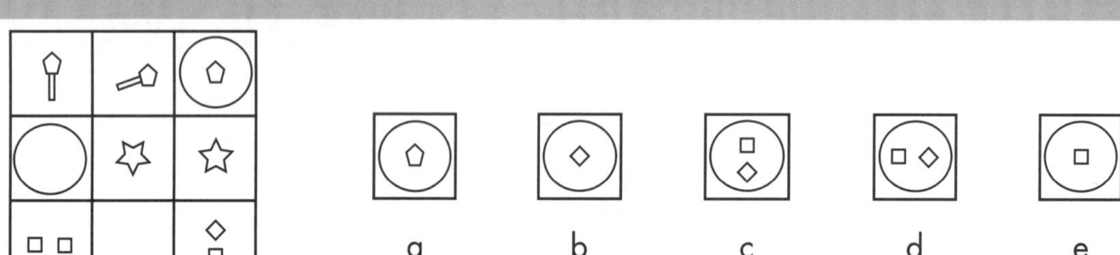

3

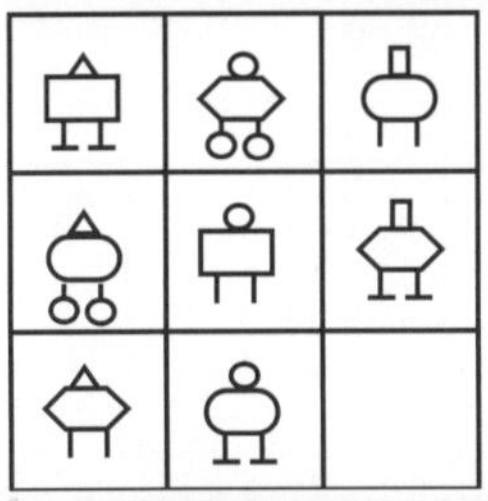

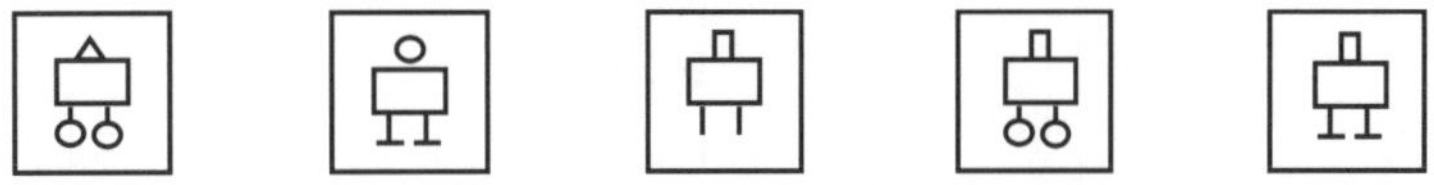

a b c d e

4

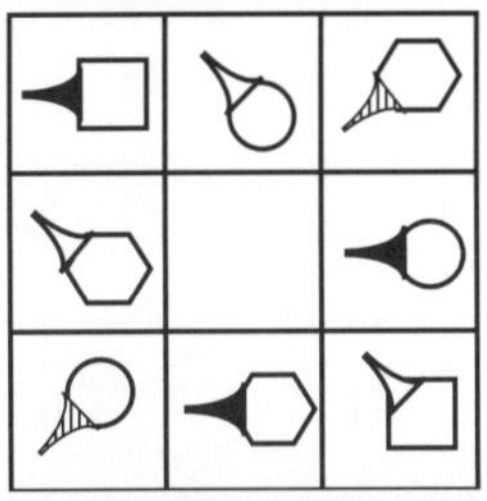

a b c d e

5

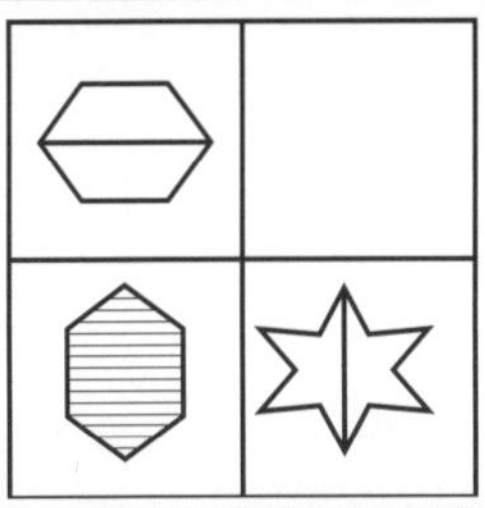

a b c d e

6

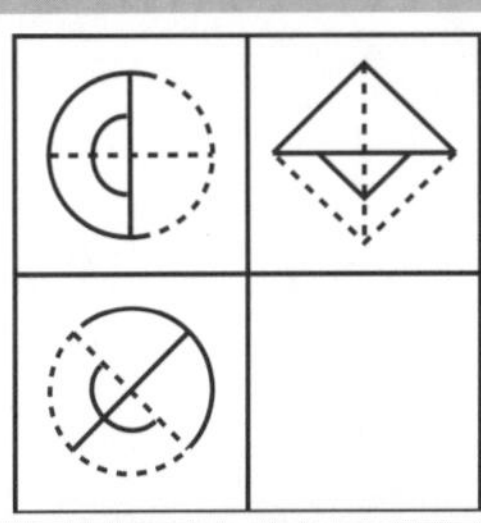

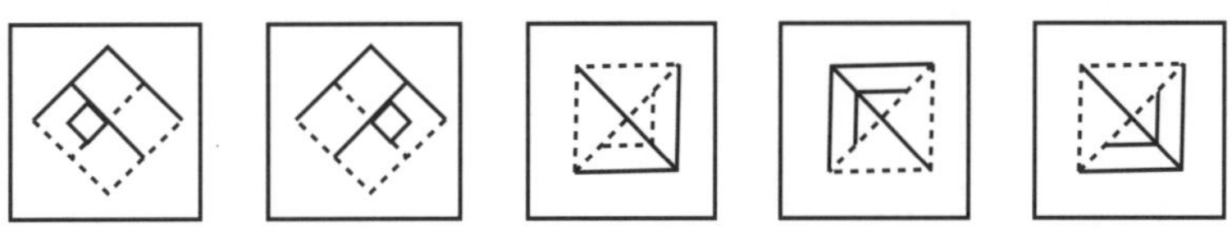

a b c d e

7

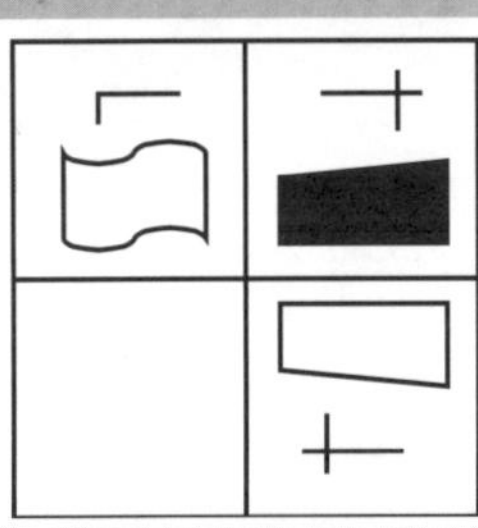

a b c d e

8

a b c d e

9

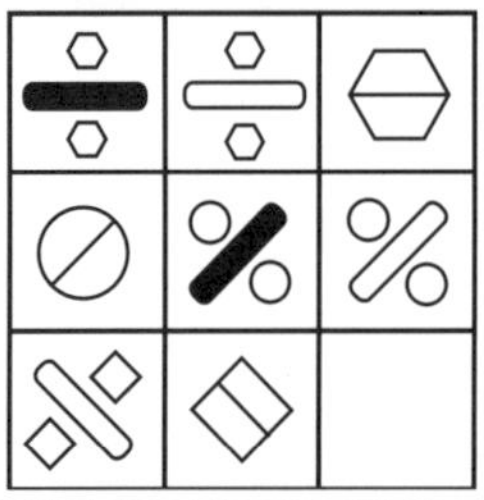

a b c d e

10

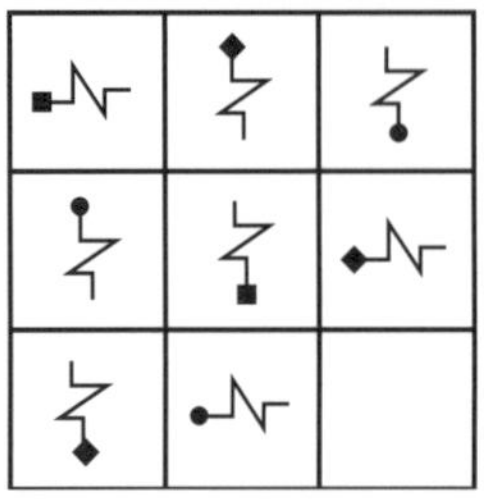

a b c d e

11

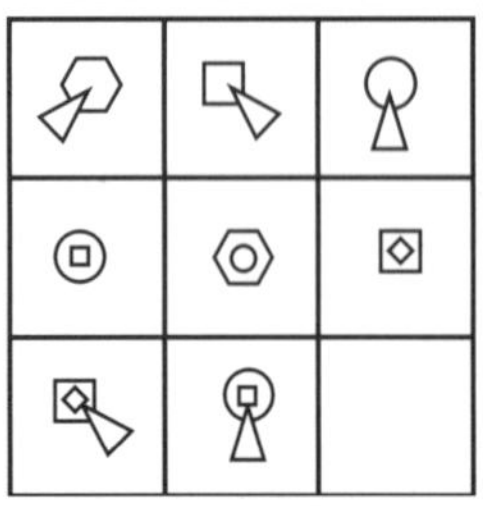

a b c d e

12

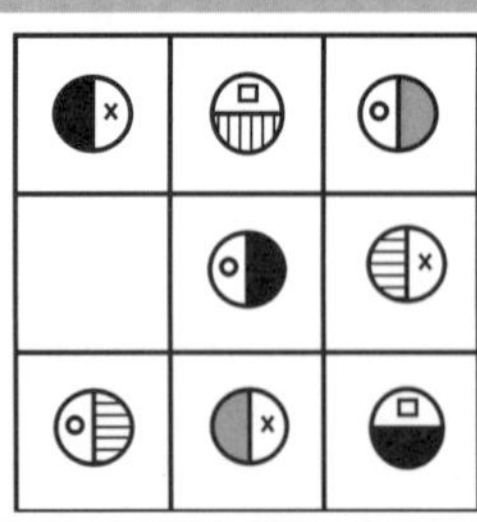

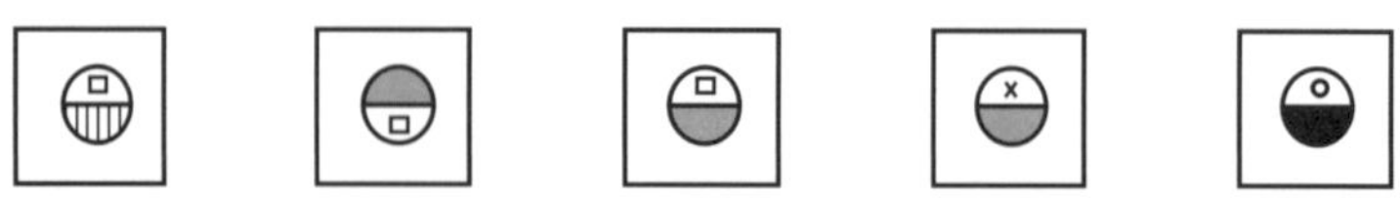

a b c d e

13

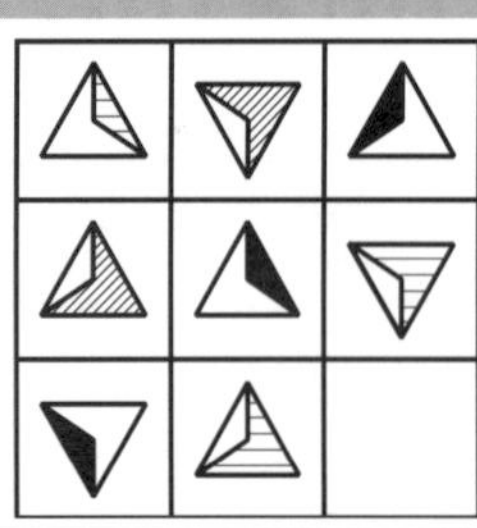

a b c d e

14

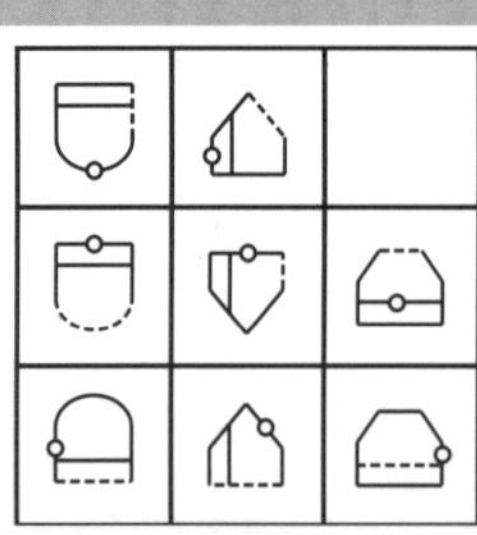

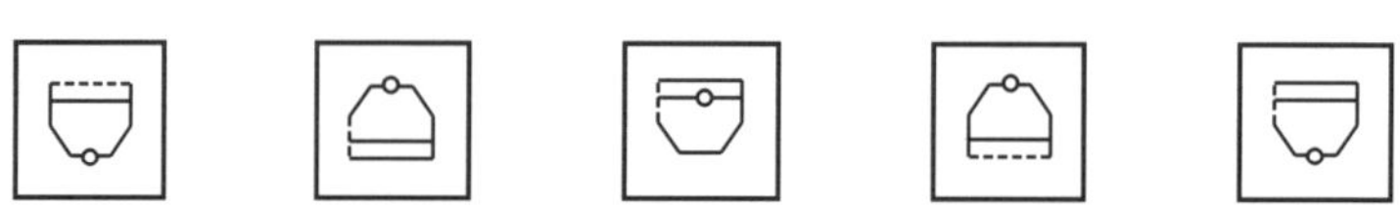

a b c d e

15

a b c d e

16

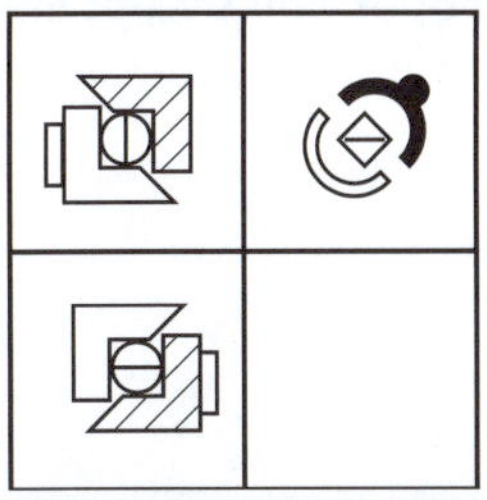

a b c d e

17

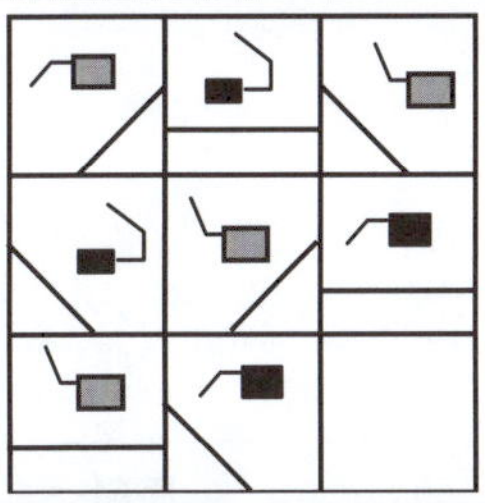

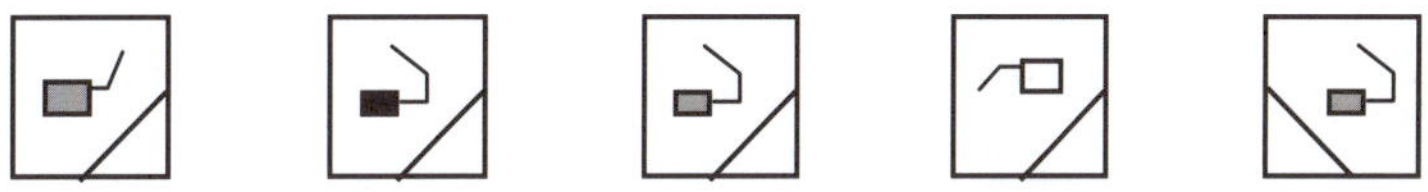

a b c d e

18

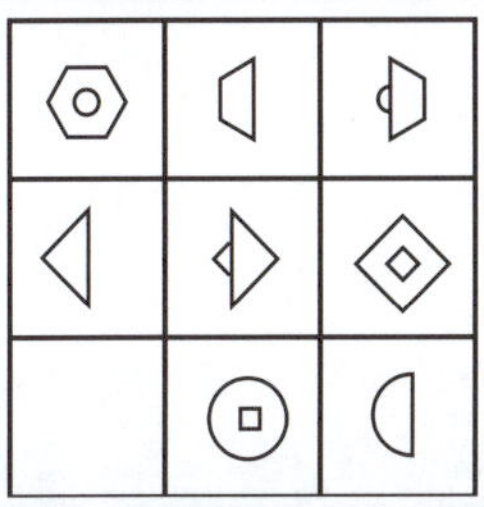

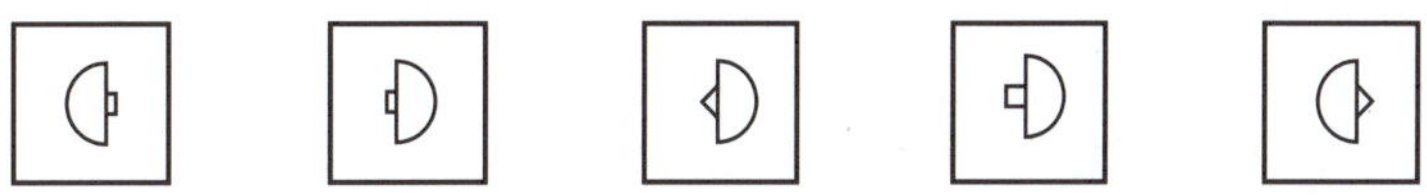

a b c d e

END OF SECTION

TYPE 3

In each question below, there are two shapes on the left hand side which are **related to each other**. To the right of the dots there is a third shape.

Pick a fourth shape from the five available options so that the third and fourth shape **share the same relationship** as the first and second shape.

Mark your choice on the multiple choice sheet.

EXAMPLE 1 EXPLANATION

1. In the first pair of shapes, the colour changes from white to black. Therefore, the shading of our shape, which is a white hexagon, must also change to black.

2. In the first pair of shapes, the first shape rotates 45° to give the second shape. Therefore, our shape must also rotate 45°.

3. In the first pair of shapes, the size of the first shape shrinks, therefore, our shape must become smaller.

EXAMPLE 1

a b c d e

EXAMPLE 2

a b c d e

START OF SECTION

19

a b c d e

20

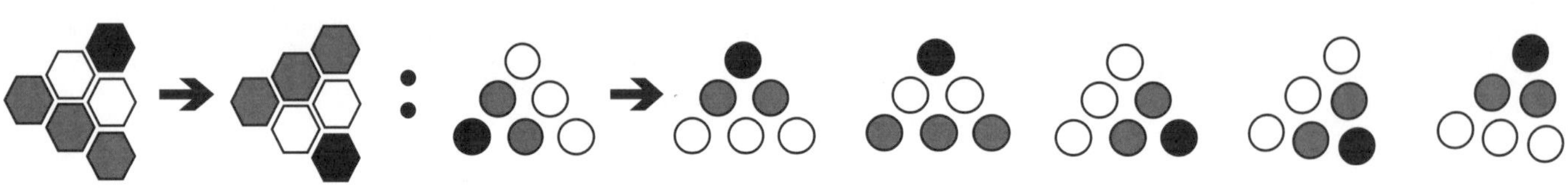

a b c d e

21

a b c d e

22

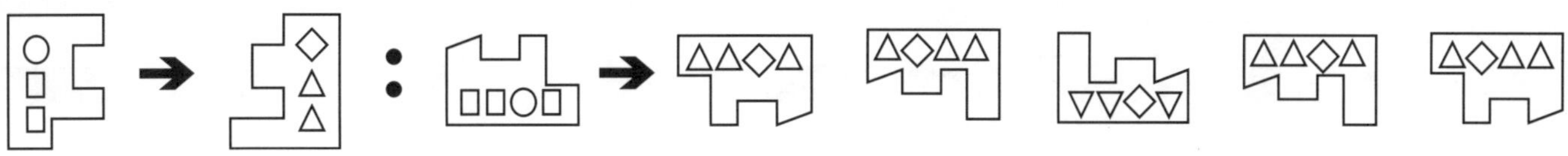

a b c d e

23

a b c d e

24

a b c d e

25

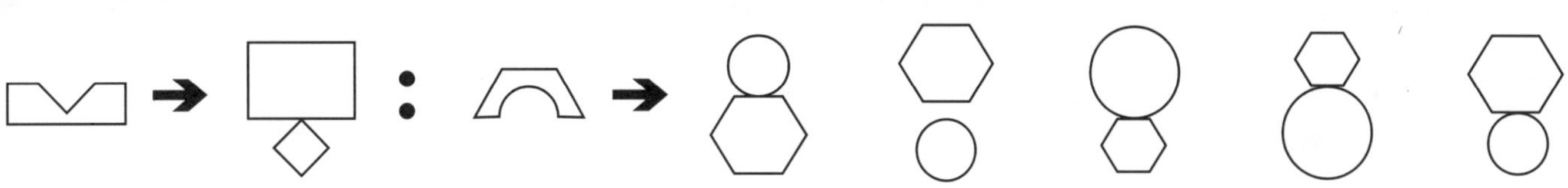

a b c d e

26

a b c d e

27

a b c d e

28

a b c d e

29

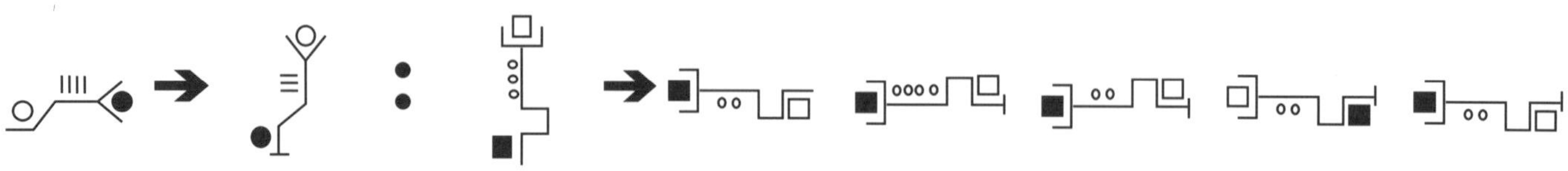

a b c d e

30

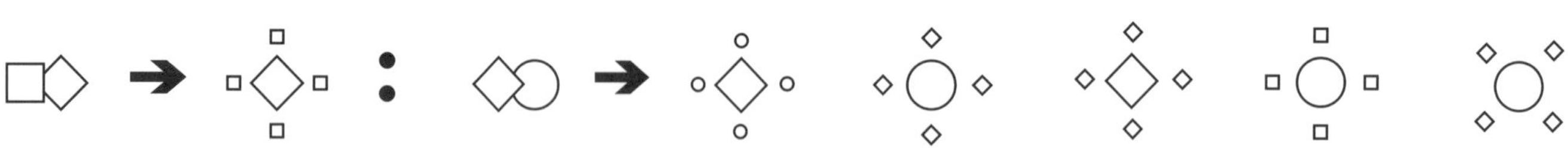

a b c d e

31

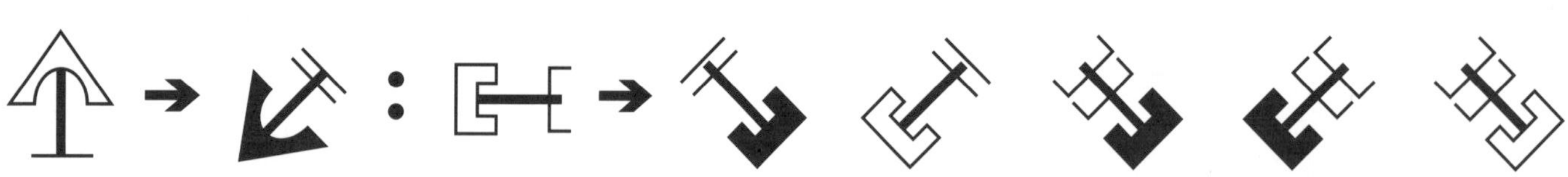

a b c d e

32

a b c d e

33

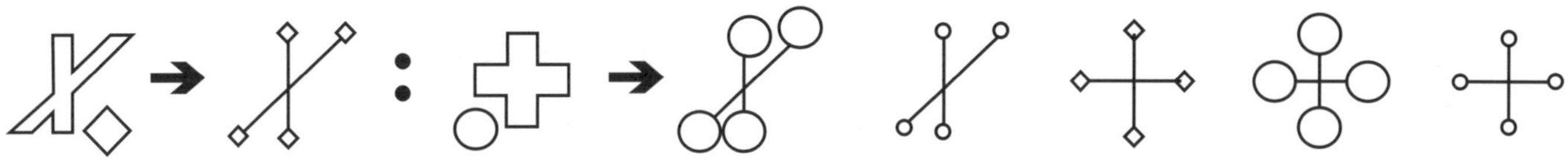

a b c d e

34

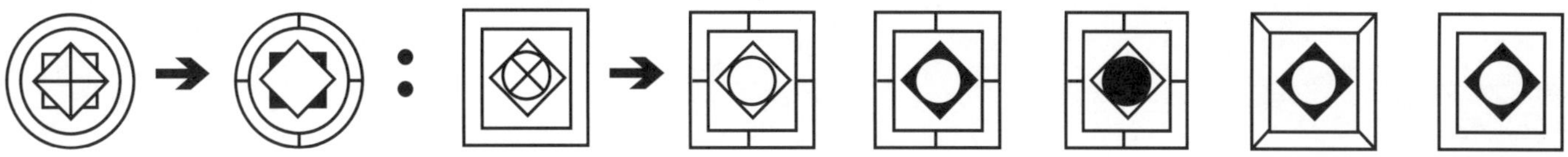

a b c d e

35

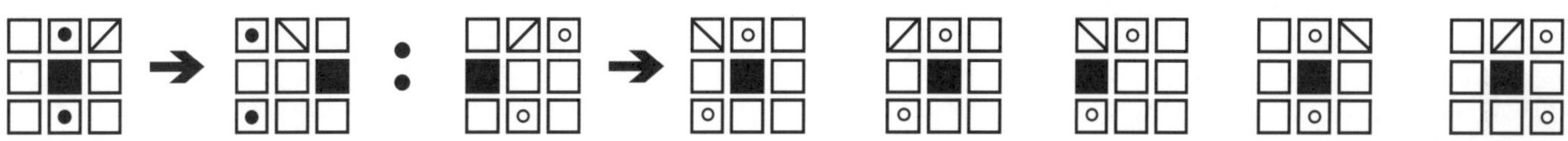

a b c d e

36

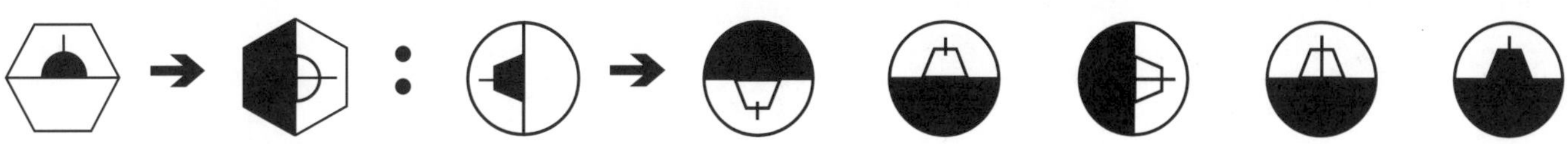

a b c d e

END OF SECTION

TYPE 4

In each question below, the shapes to the left of the vertical line are similar in a number of ways.

Select the shape from the five provided on the right which is the **most similar** to the shapes on the left.

Mark your answer on the multiple choice sheet.

EXAMPLE 1 EXPLANATION

1. Both shapes to the left of the black line contain a white rectangle. Therefore, the answer cannot be **b** as it does not contain a white rectangle, but instead has a square.

2. Both shapes to the left of black line also contain a black diamond. Therefore, the answer is **d**, as it is the only choice containing both a black diamond and a white rectangle.

EXAMPLE 1

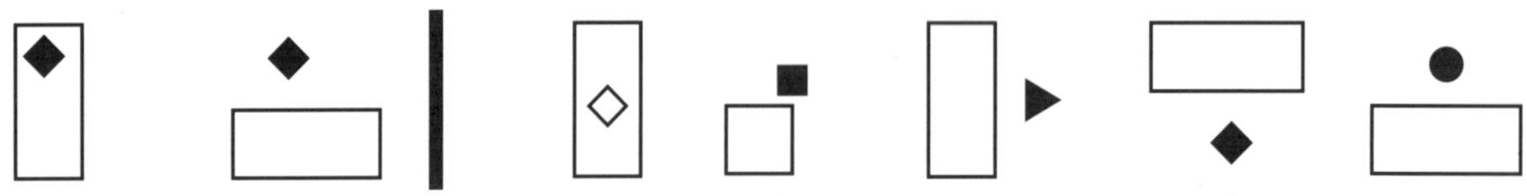

a b c **d** e

EXAMPLE 2

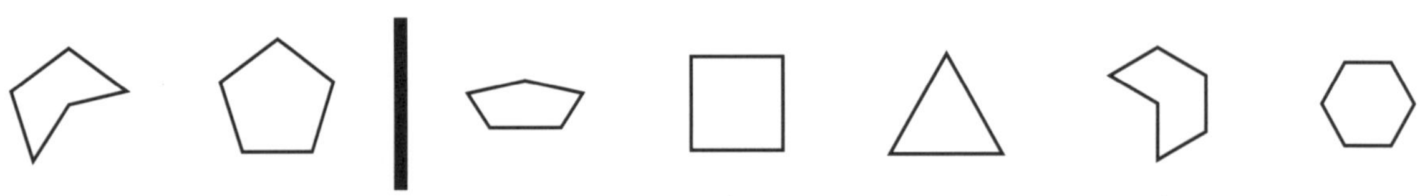

a b c d e

START OF SECTION

37

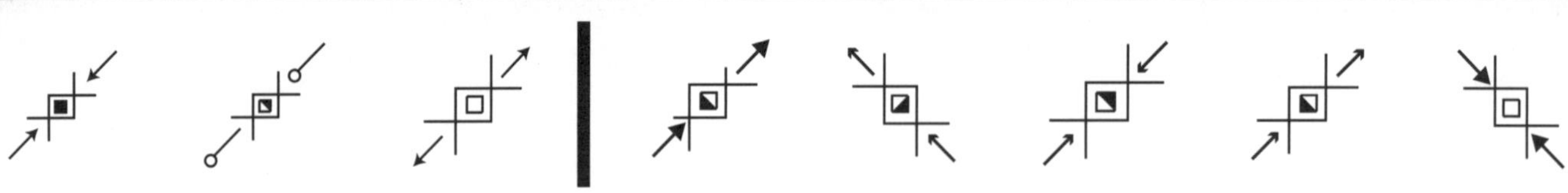

a b c d e

38

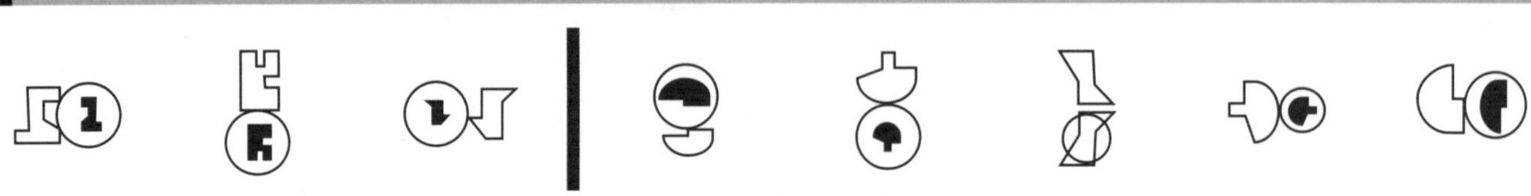

a b c d e

39

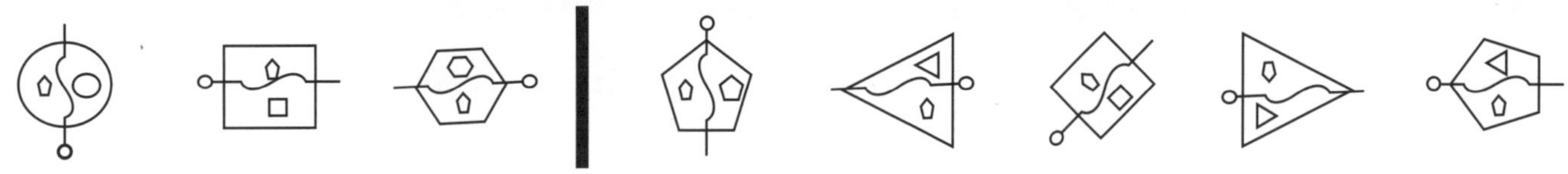

a b c d e

40

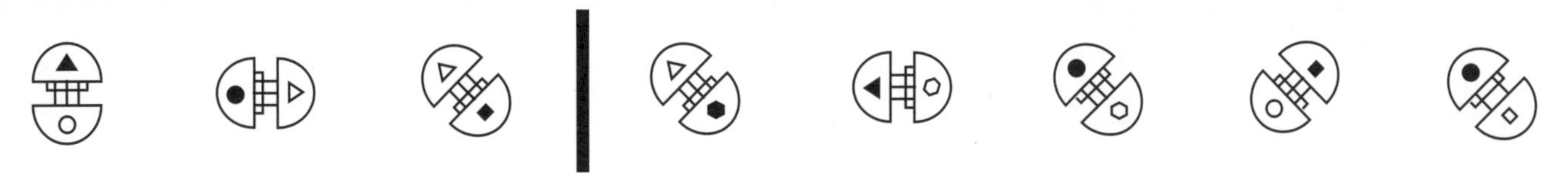

a b c d e

41

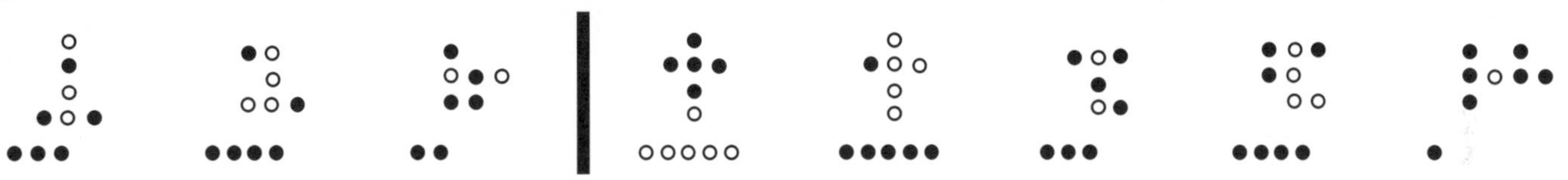

a b c d e

42

a b c d e

43

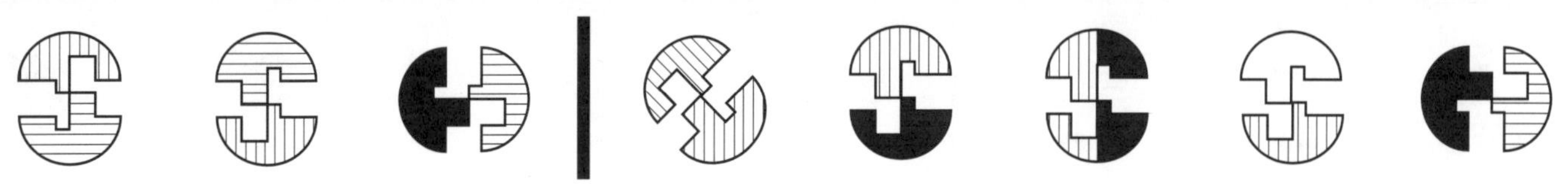

a b c d e

44

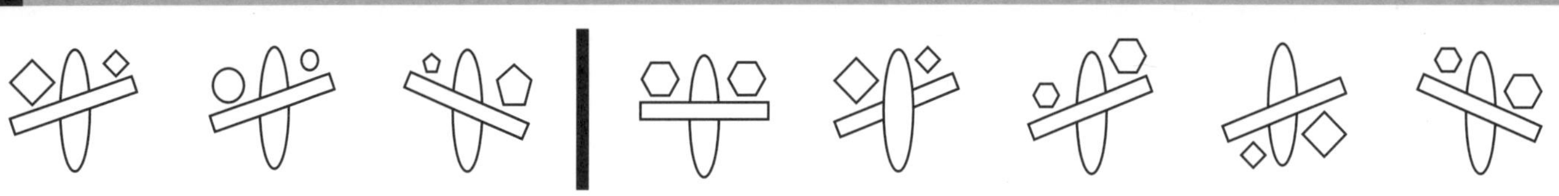

a b c d e

45

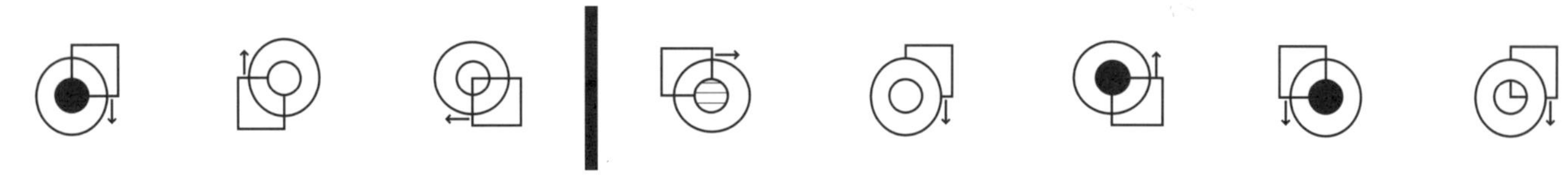

a b c d e

46

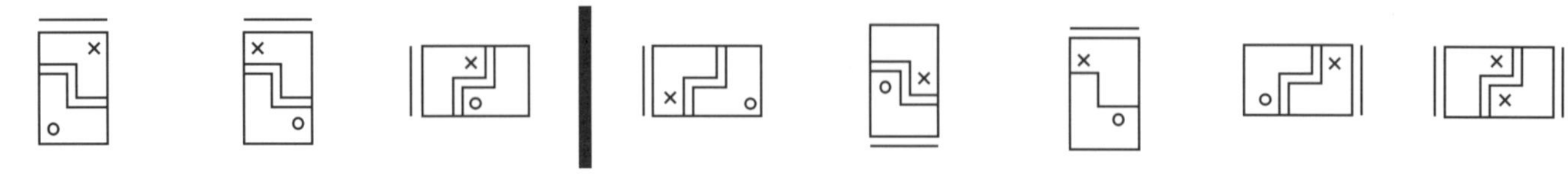

a b c d e

47

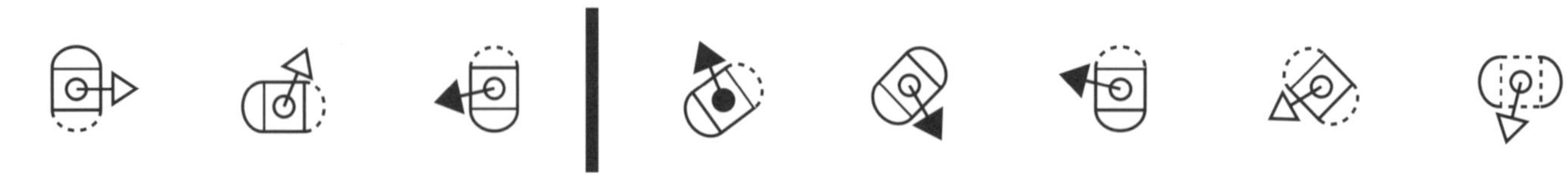

a b c d e

48

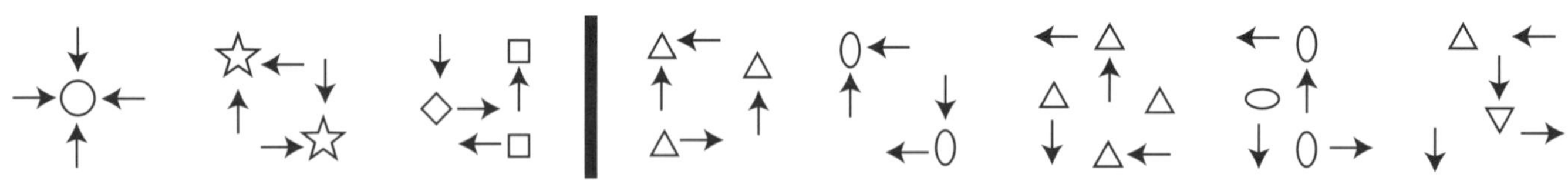

a b c d e

49

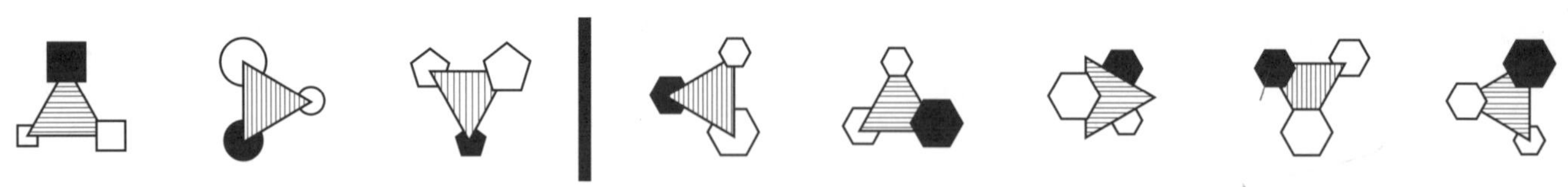

a b c d e

50

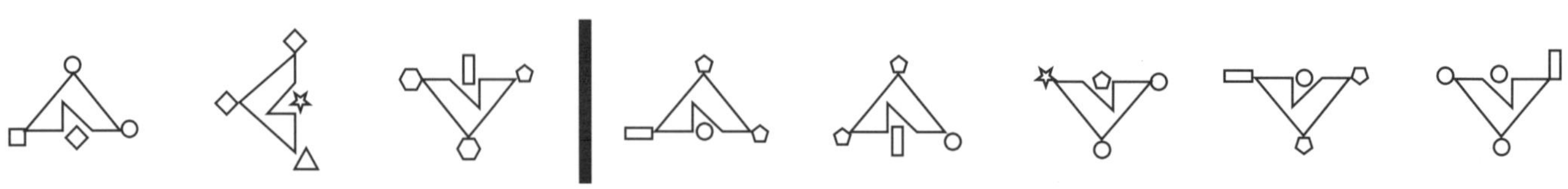

a b c d e

51

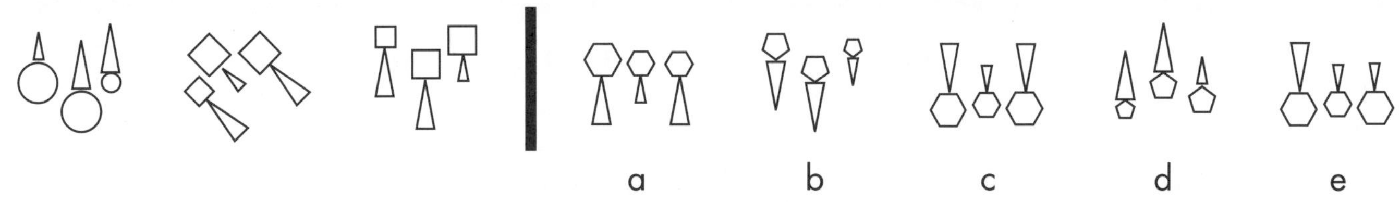

52

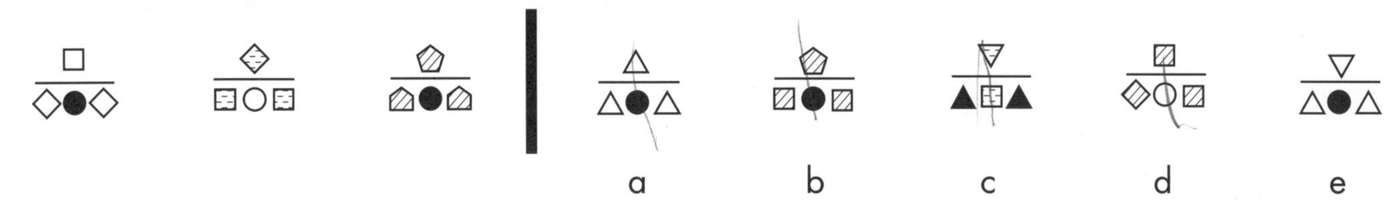

53

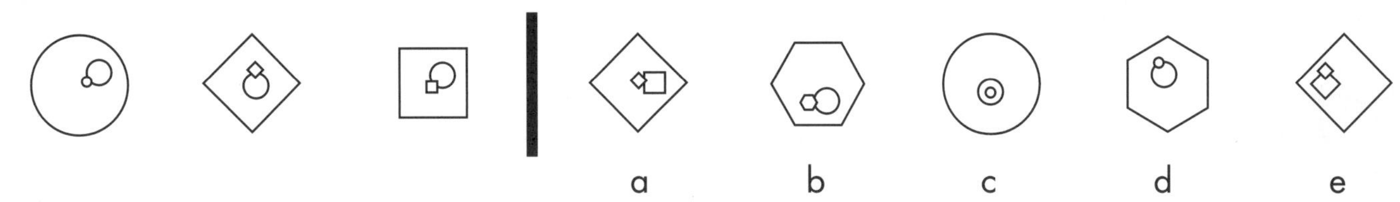

54

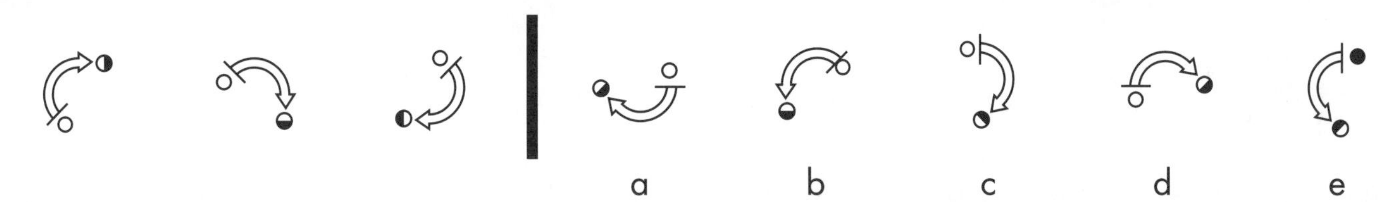

END OF SECTION

TYPE 5

In each question below, the shapes on the left have been identified with a code. Each letter in the code represents a **different characteristic** of the shapes.

By working out what the letters mean, you must select the correct code to **describe the new shape** you have been given.

Select the correct code from the five options on the right and mark its letter on the multiple choice sheet.

EXAMPLE 1 EXPLANATION

1. The first and last figure are the same shape and share the same first letter. The first letter, therefore, represents the shape of the figure so the first letter for our figure is D.

2. The first shape and the third shape are black and share the same second letter, therefore, the second letter represents shading. Our shape has the same shading as the second shape, so its second letter must be S.

EXAMPLE 1

DR
ES
GR
DG

ER	EG	GG	DS	GS
a	b	c	d	e

EXAMPLE 2

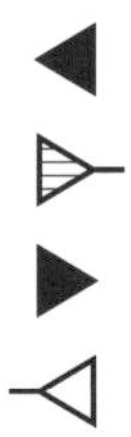

EDW
GSR
ESW
BDR

GDW	BSR	GDR	BSW	EDR
a	b	c	d	e

START OF SECTION

55

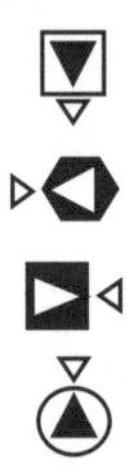

MRE
LTF
MSF
NQF

LQE	MTF	LRE	NRE	LRF
a	b	c	d	e

56

BS
BA
CA
CE

CE	CS	CA	BE	BS
a	b	c	d	e

57

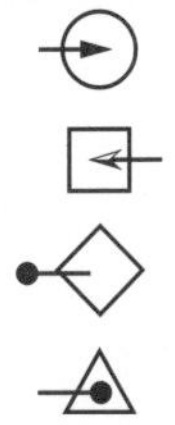

AX
BY
CZ
DZ

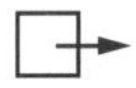

AY	DX	BX	BZ	AZ
a	b	c	d	e

58

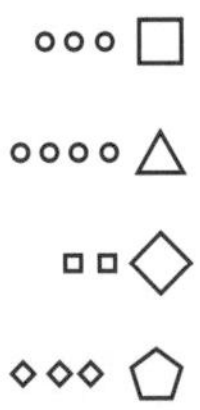

CYT
AST
MYL
CJG

CJT	AYG	MJG	AJL	AJT
a	b	c	d	e

59

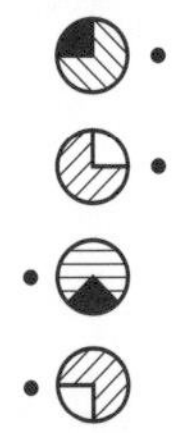

PA
NL
RB
ML

RL	PB	PL	RA	MA
a	b	c	d	e

60

PLM
OLN
PHB
VJM

OLB	OHM	OJB	VHB	VJN
a	b	c	d	e

61

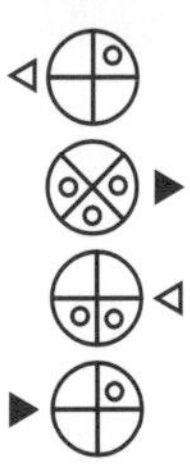

WER
FGR
WNP
WEP

WGP	FEP	FNP	FGP	FNR
a	b	c	d	e

62

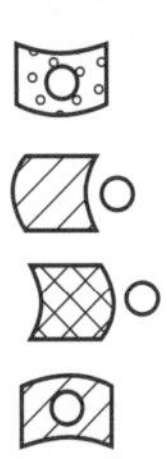

ATN
BML
KOP
AXL

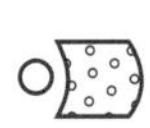

AOP	KON	KTP	BON	BMN
a	b	c	d	e

63

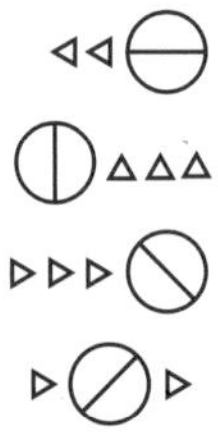

WSX
RFV
WGB
TGN

a	b	c	d	e
TFX	TSB	RSV	RSB	RGX

64

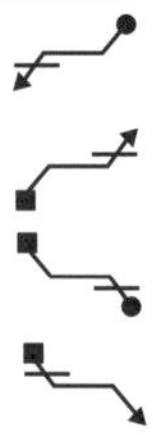

JKL
FGL
AGS
EOR

a	b	c	d	e
JGR	FOS	FGS	JOS	AOR

65

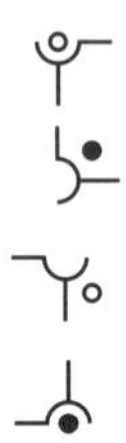

ASD
ZXC
VBD
ATC

a	b	c	d	e
ZXC	ZBC	ABD	AXC	VBC

66

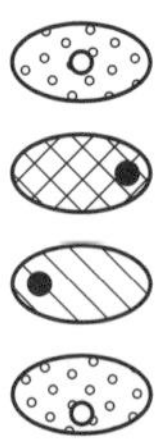

PL
AS
DF
PB

a	b	c	d	e
DB	PS	DS	PF	DL

67

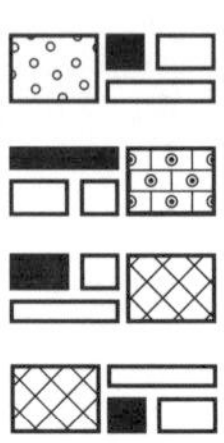

POI
UYT
REW
RCI

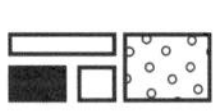

a	b	c	d	e
PYT	PYW	PET	UYW	UOT

68

YAT
RAE
YBV
RAM

a	b	c	d	e
YBE	YAV	YBM	RBE	RAT

69

 AX
 BY
 AZ
 BV

a	b	c	d	e
BX	AY	BV	AV	BZ

70

 AX
 BY
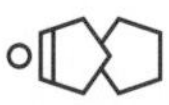 ZX

a	b	c	d	e
BX	BY	ZY	AY	ZX

71

 AWE
 AVN
 BWJ

a	b	c	d	e
BVE	AVJ	AWN	BVJ	BWN

72

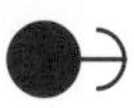 BT
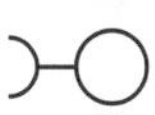 FV
 ST
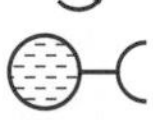 AV

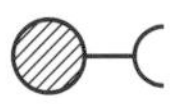

a	b	c	d	e
BV	ST	SV	AT	AV

END OF TEST

[THIS PAGE IS INTENTIONALLY LEFT BLANK]

[THIS PAGE IS INTENTIONALLY LEFT BLANK]

NON VERBAL
TEST 11

Read the following instructions carefully:

1. Do not open this question booklet until you are instructed to do so.

2. This test has four sections, each containing 18 questions. There are 72 questions in total.

3. All your answers must be marked on the separate multiple choice sheet. Answers written on this question booklet will not be counted.

4. You may write any rough working on this question booklet.

5. For all questions you must select only one answer.

6. To mark your answer, draw a horizontal line through the rectangle next to your answer on the multiple choice sheet. If you want to change your answer, rub it out as completely as you can and then select your new answer.

7. Make sure you do not lose your place on the multiple choice sheet. Check that your answer box has the same number as the question that you are on.

8. You may not get to the end of the paper, but complete as many questions as you can. If a question is taking you too long, make sure you do not waste time on it and move forward to the next question. If you cannot decide which is the correct answer, select the one you think is most likely to be correct.

9. You have 50 minutes to complete this test. Work as quickly and carefully as you can.

Authors: Steven Vu and Graham Wildash

Published by Test Teach Limited.
Unit 203 Kingspark Business Centre, 152-178 Kingston Road, Kingston Upon Thames, KT3 3ST.

Test Teach

DO NOT OPEN THIS BOOKLET UNTIL TOLD TO DO SO

TYPE 7

In each question, five boxes have been **arranged in a sequence**. One box has been removed so that the sequence is no longer complete.

From the five options on the right, **find which box has been removed** and mark its letter on your multiple choice sheet.

EXAMPLE 1 EXPLANATION

1. The central shape is alternating in colour and shape. Our missing box, therefore, must contain a central shape which is a black square.

2. There is a small black square located in one of the corners in each box. It moves clockwise from corner to corner. Therefore, our missing box must also contain a small black square in its top left corner.

EXAMPLE 1

a b c d e

EXAMPLE 2

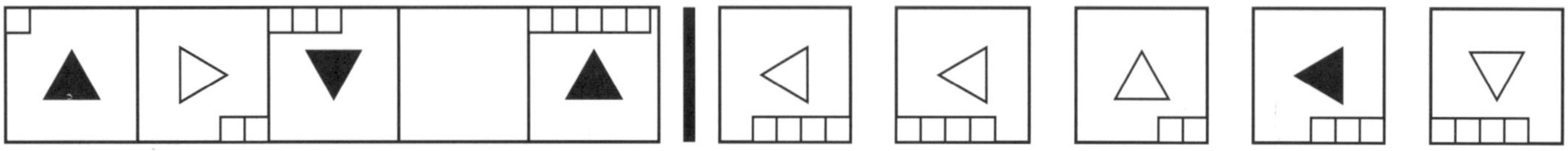

a b c d e

START OF SECTION

1

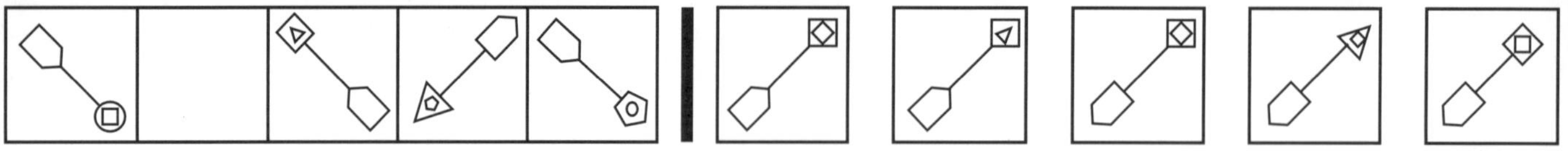

a b c d e

2

a b c d e

3

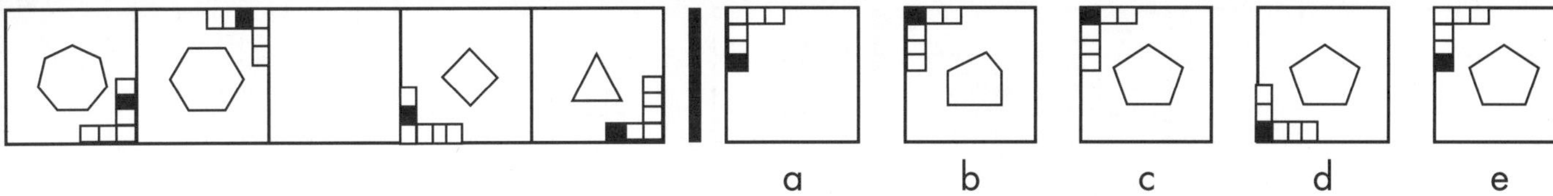

4

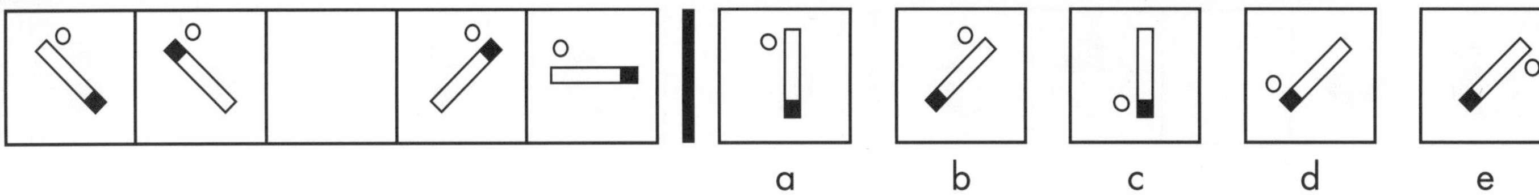

5

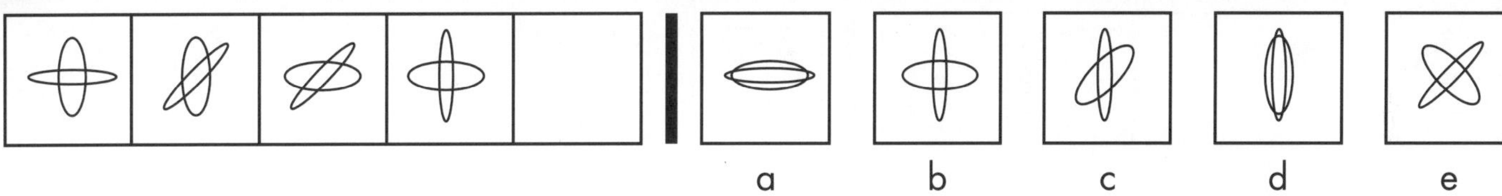

6

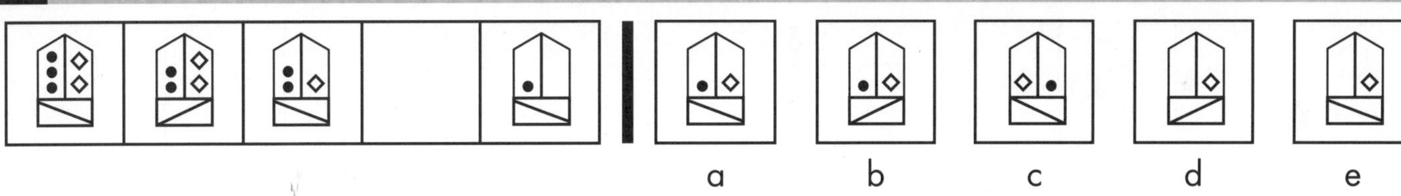

7

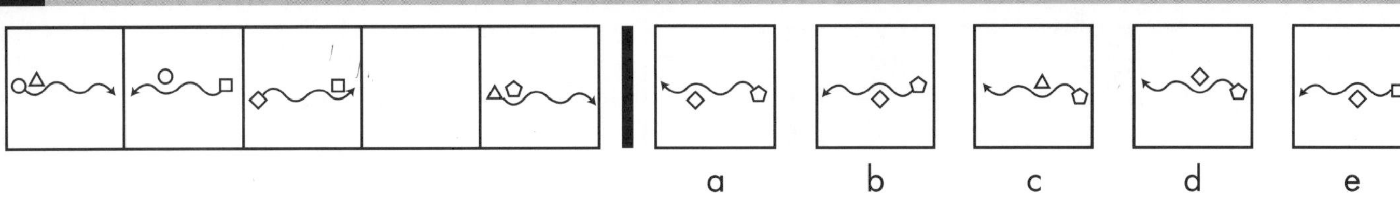

8

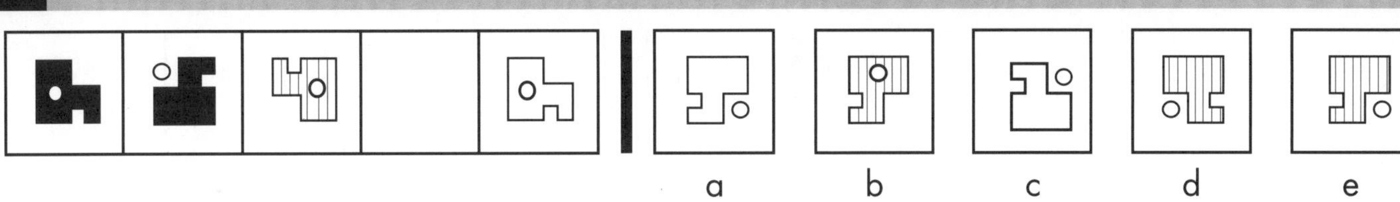

9

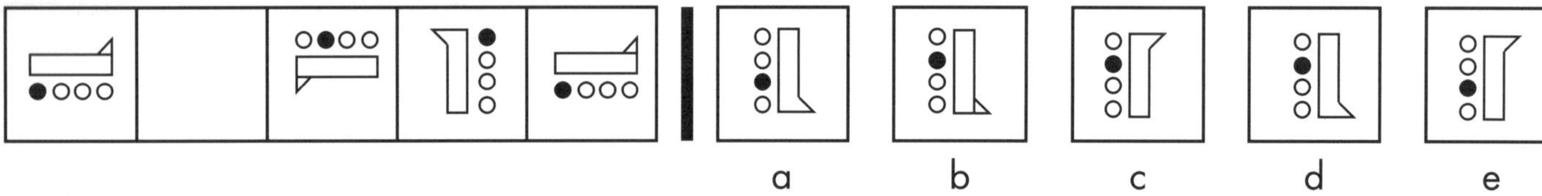

10

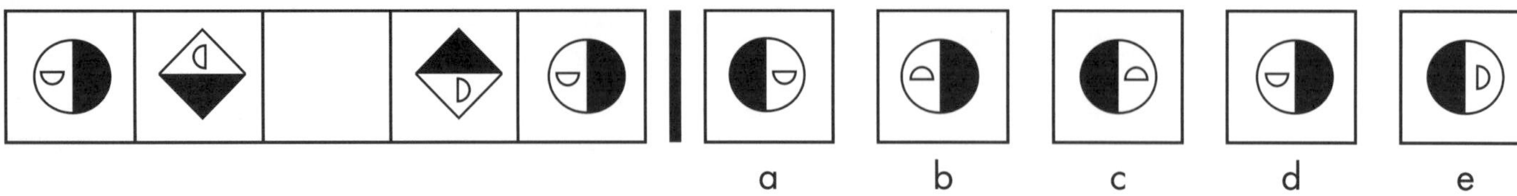

11

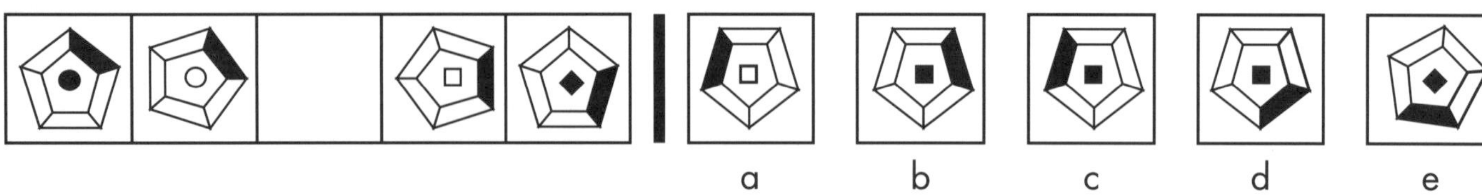

12

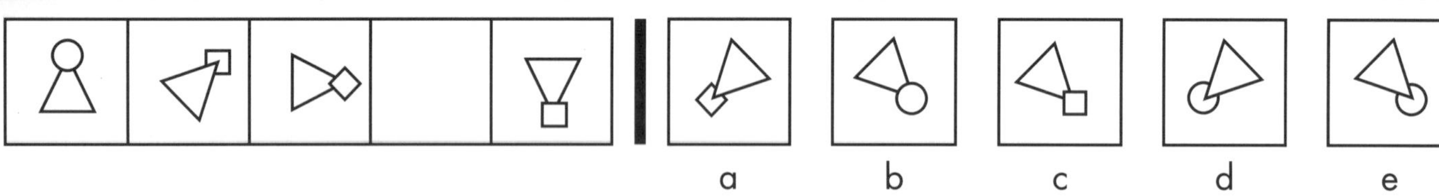

13

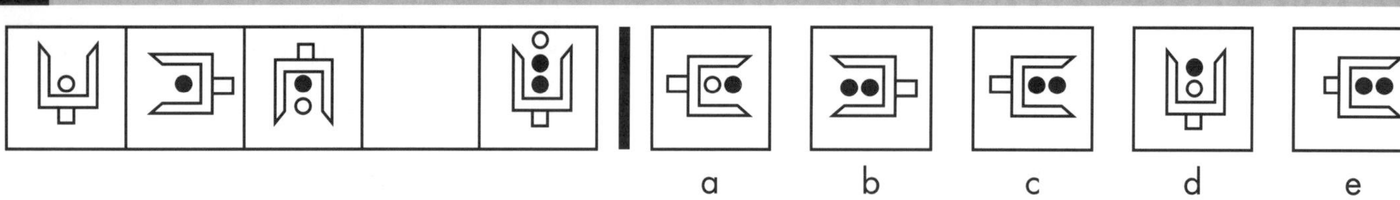

14

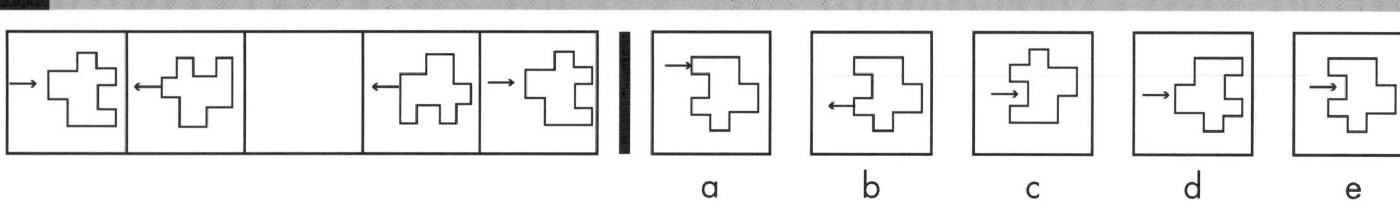

15

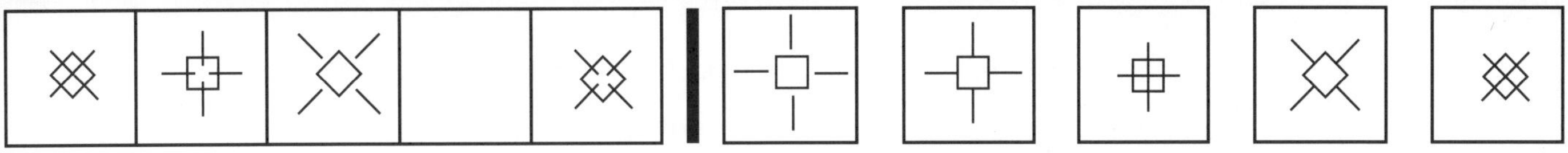

a b c d e

16

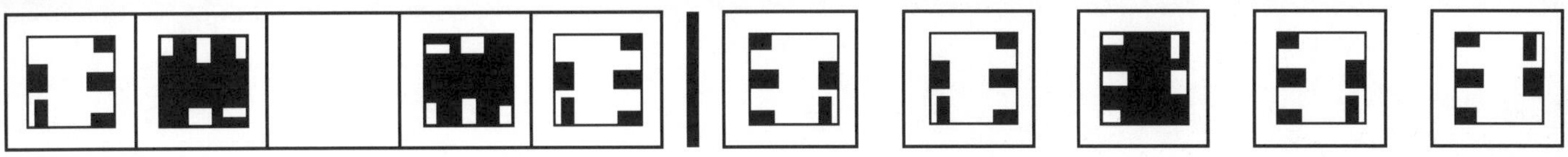

a b c d e

17

a b c d e

18

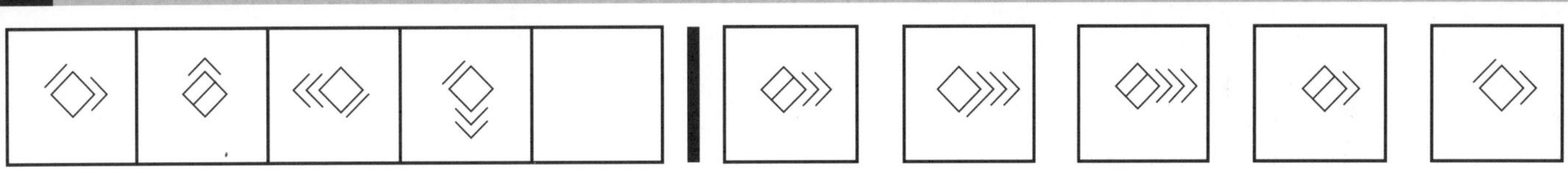

a b c d e

END OF SECTION

TYPE 6

In each question below, there are four boxes that have been identified with a two-letter code. The **top letters represent one characteristic** of the shapes contained within the boxes, the **bottom letters represent another**.

By working out what the letters represent, you must select the correct two-letter code to **describe the shape** found in the box to the right of the black line.

Mark your answer on the multiple choice sheet.

EXAMPLE 1 EXPLANATION

1. Boxes one and three share the same top letter and also contain shapes which are black. The top letter, therefore, represents the shading of the shape. Our shape is striped vertically, the same as the second shape, so its top letter must be E.

2. Boxes three and four share the same bottom letter and both contain shapes that point upwards. Our shape also points upwards, so the bottom letter of our box is C.

EXAMPLE 1

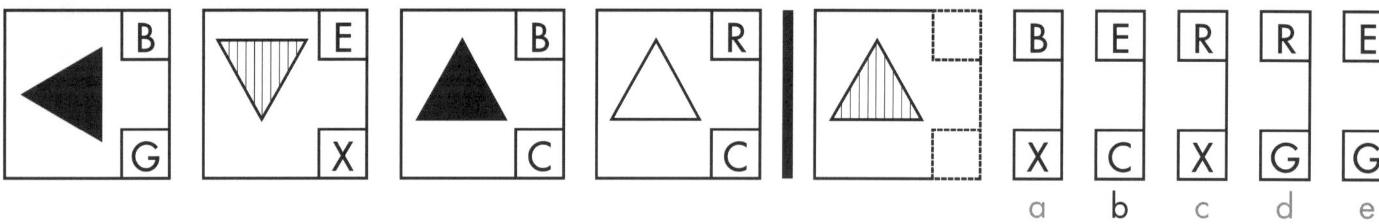

EXAMPLE 2

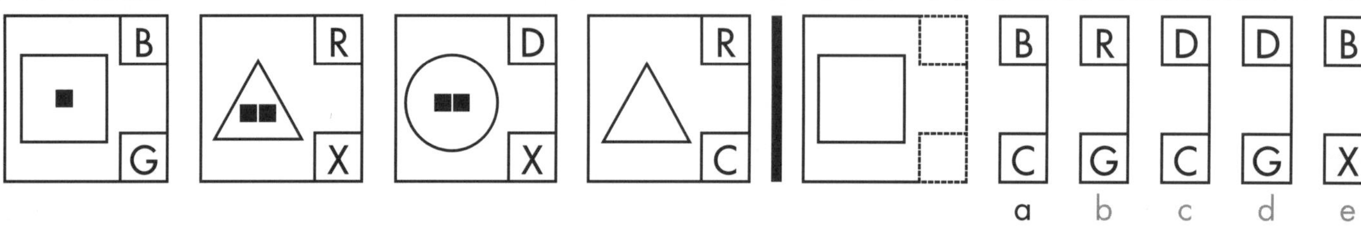

START OF SECTION

19

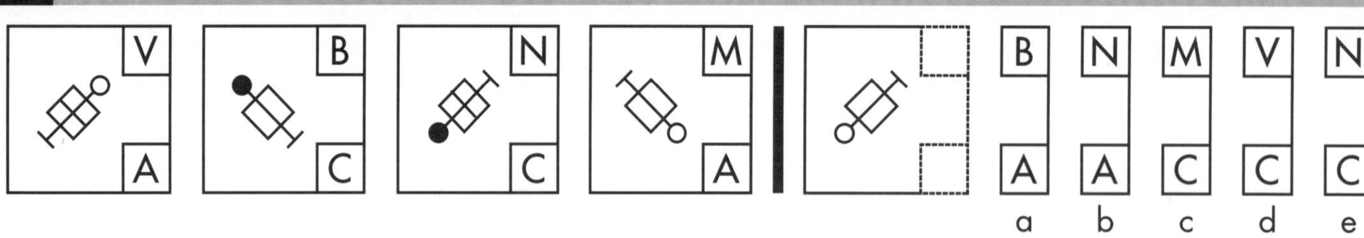

20

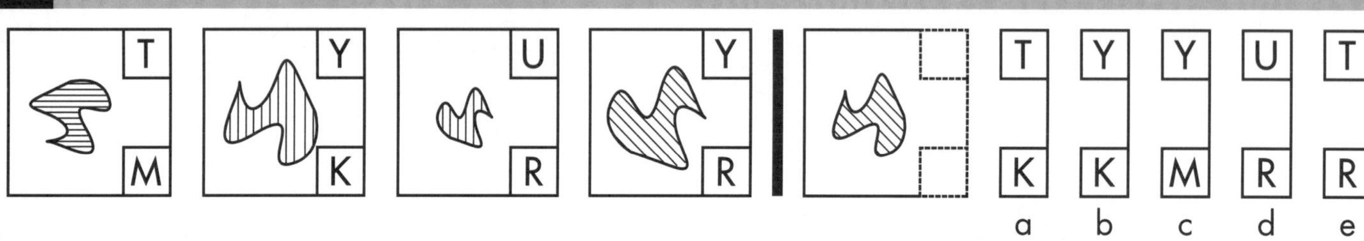

21

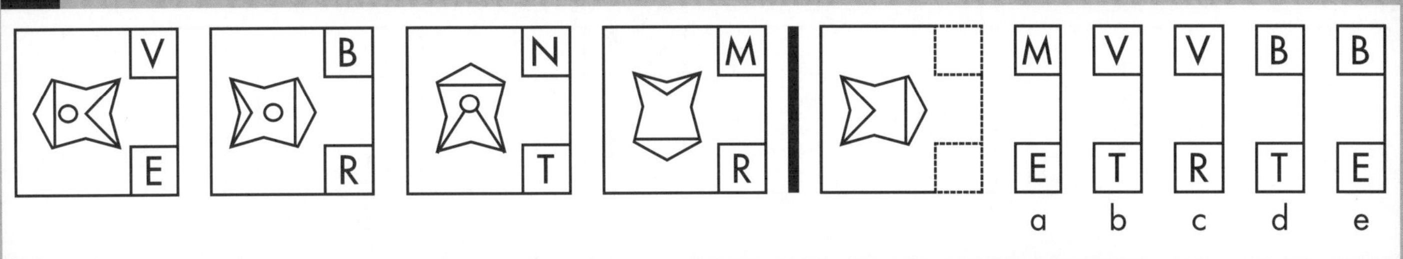

22

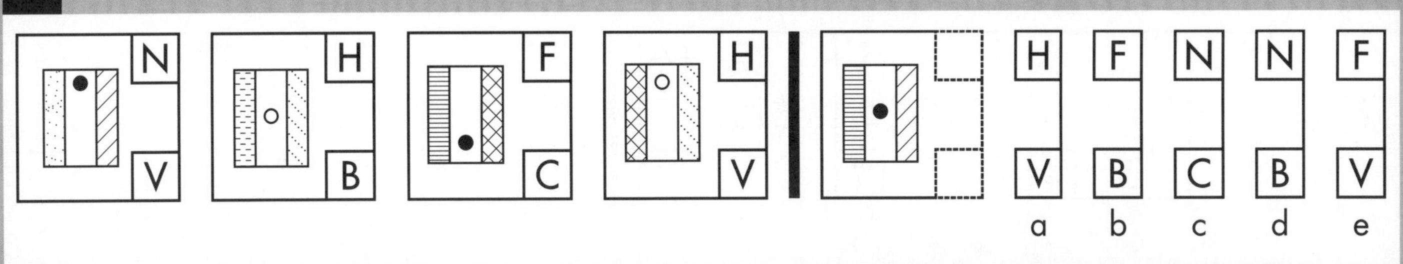

23

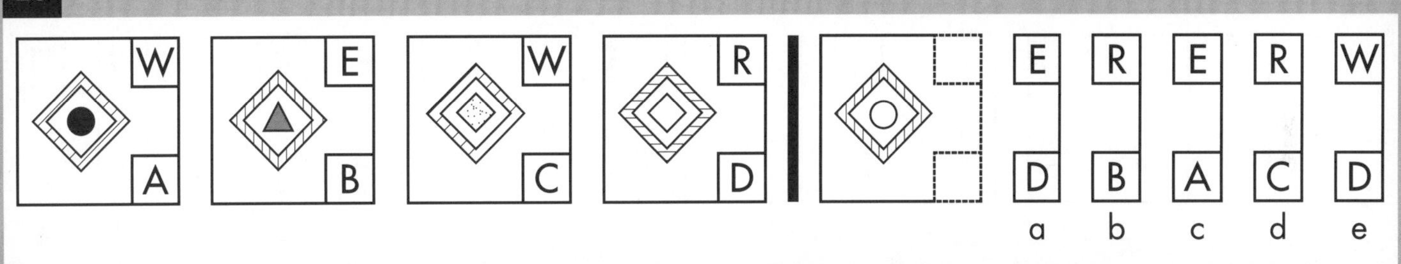

24

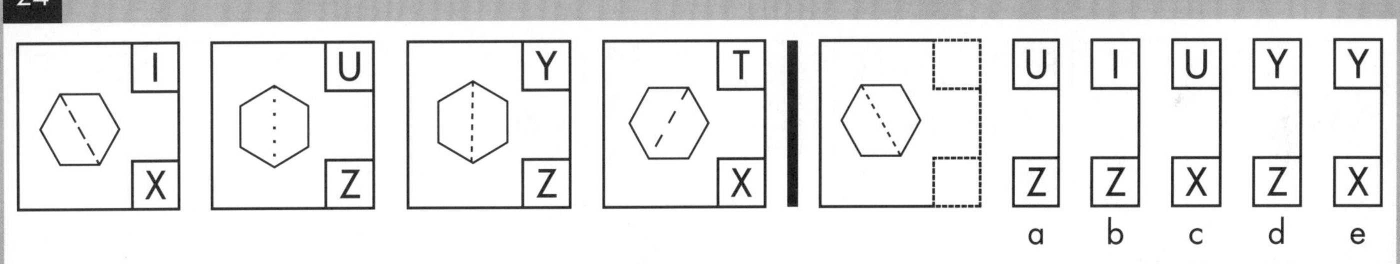

25

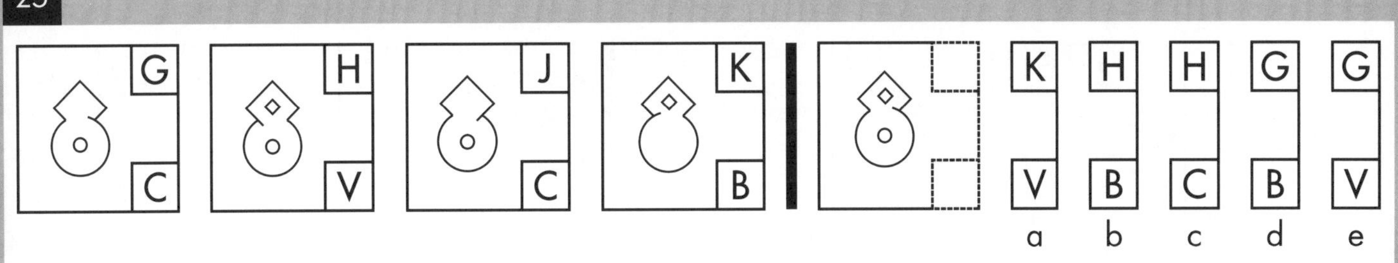

26

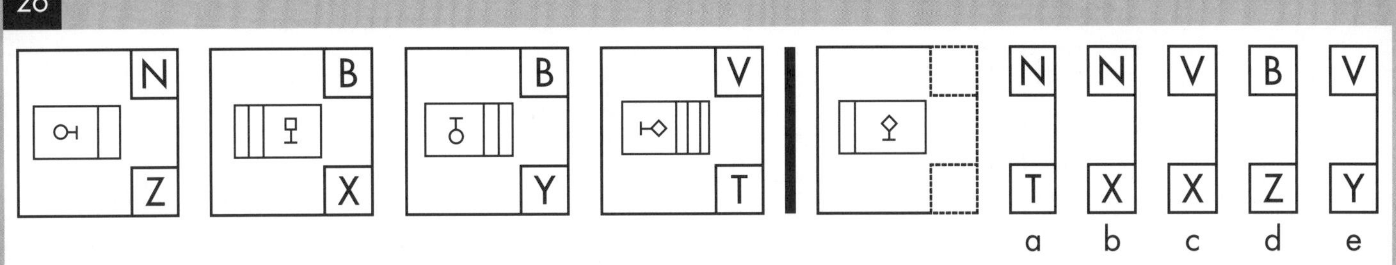

27

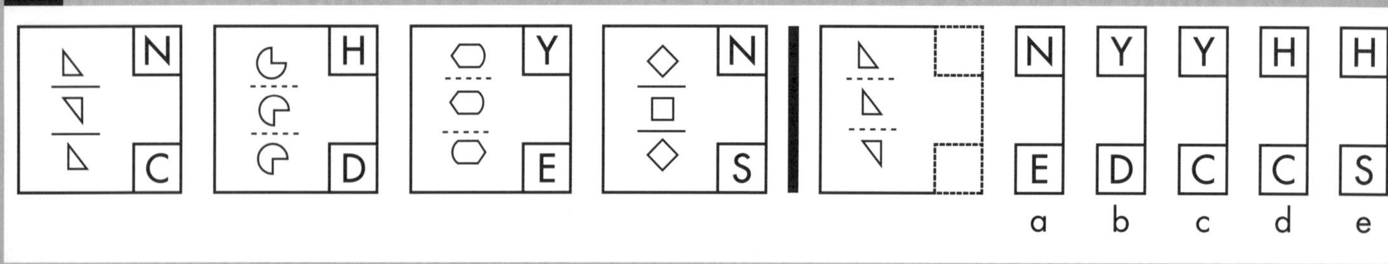

28

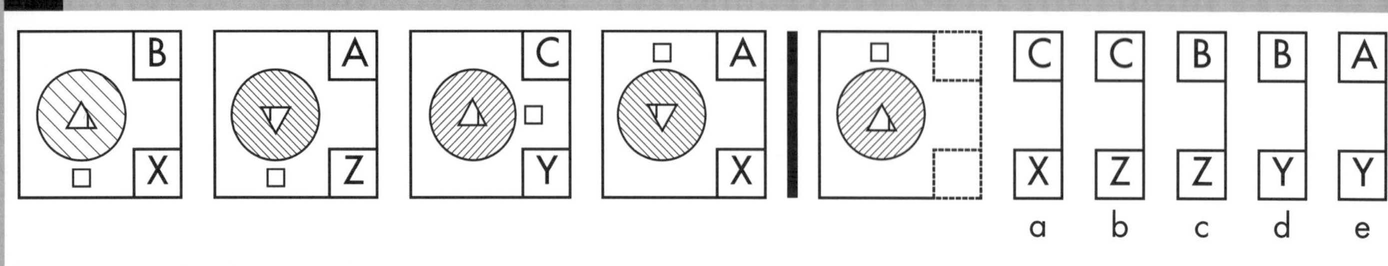

29

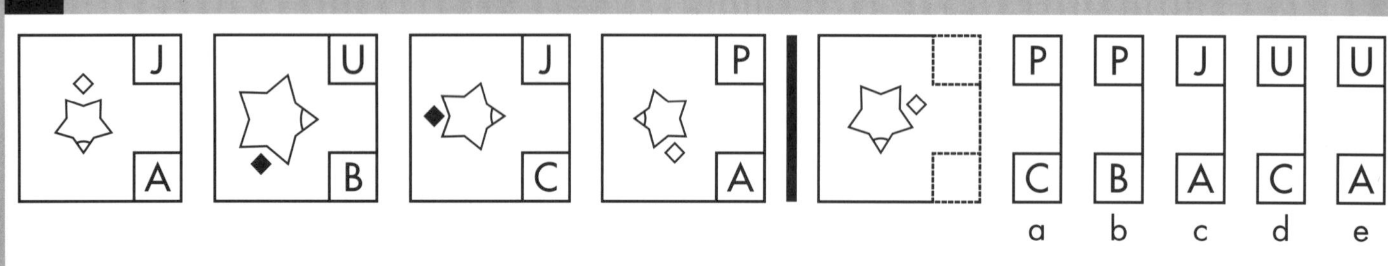

30

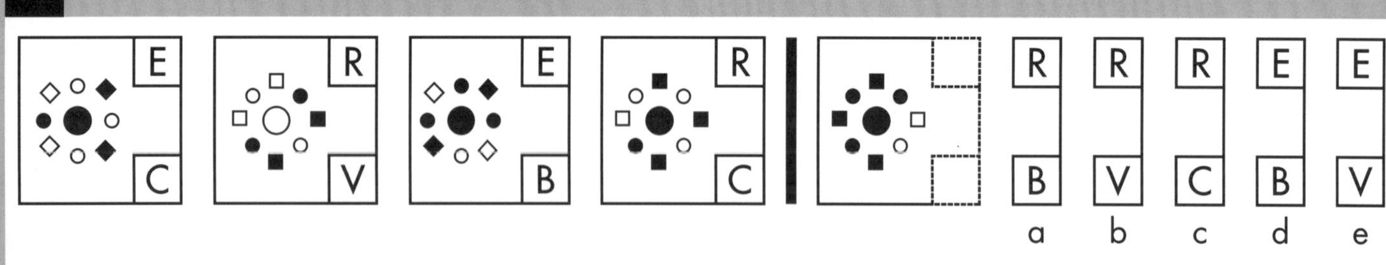

31

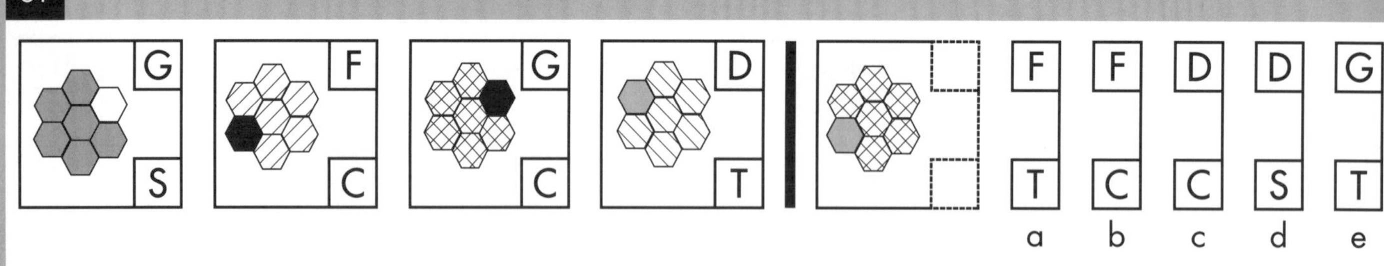

32

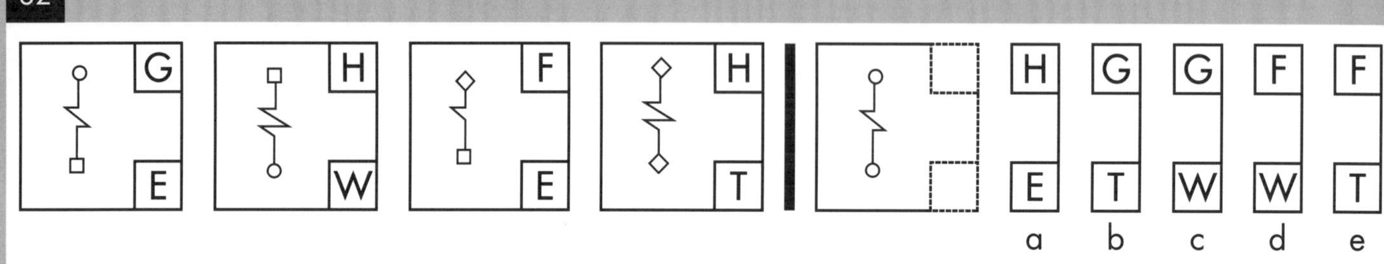

33

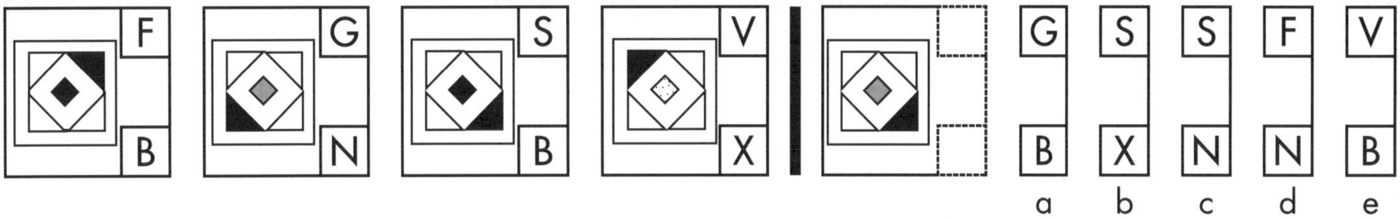

34

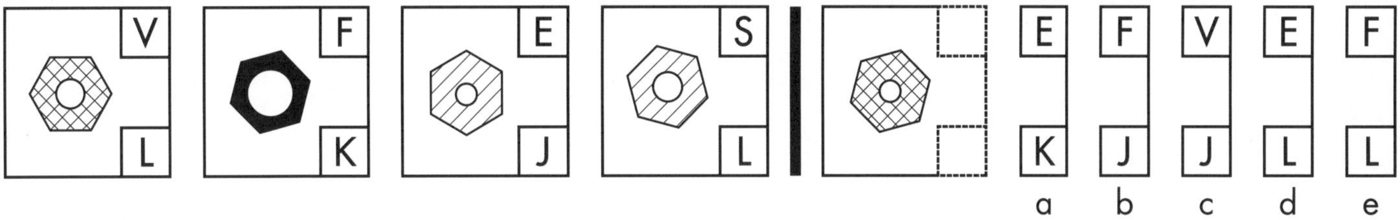

35

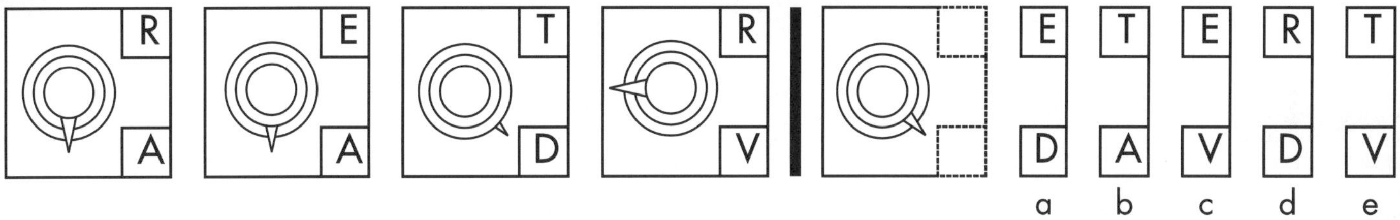

36

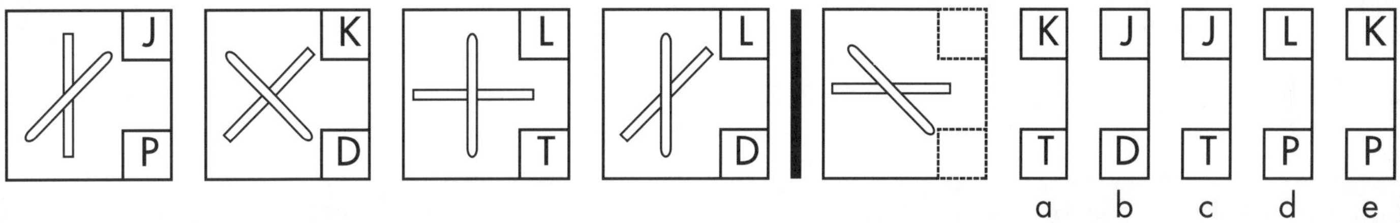

END OF SECTION

TYPE 1

In each question below, there is a grid which contains **one empty square**.

Determine which figure is missing from the empty square and mark its letter on your multiple choice sheet.

EXAMPLE 1 EXPLANATION

1. Each row contains figures of the same colour and shape. The missing square is in the top row and, therefore, must contain a black triangle.

2. Each column contains shapes of the same size. The missing square must, therefore, contain a large shape.

3. Having determined the logic that governs the rows and columns, we can now deduce that our shape must be a large black triangle.

EXAMPLE 1

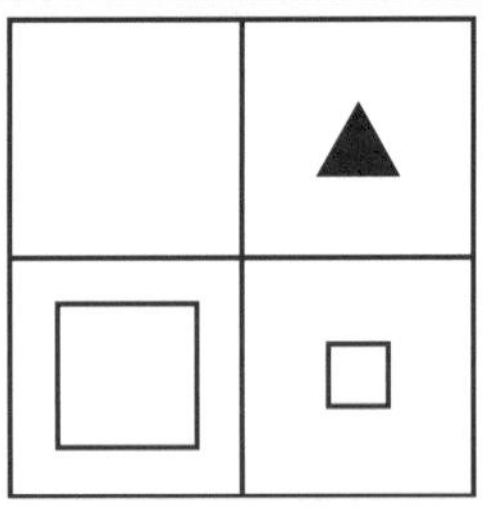

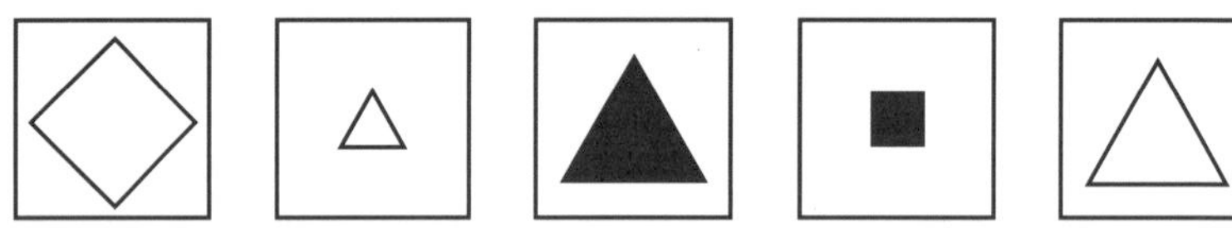

a b c d e

EXAMPLE 2

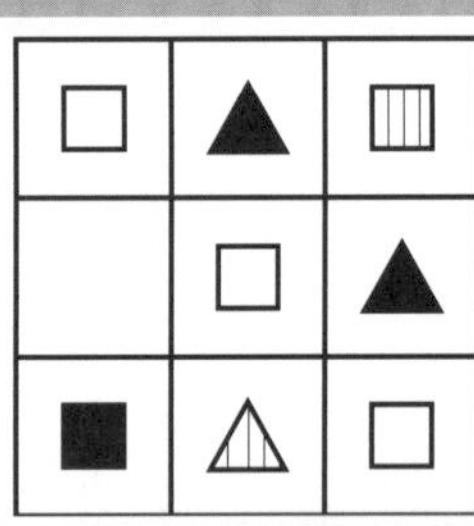

a b c d e

START OF SECTION

37

a b c d e

38

a b c d e

39

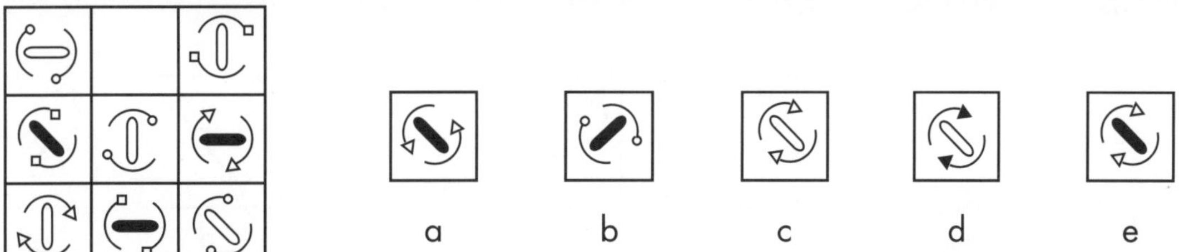

40

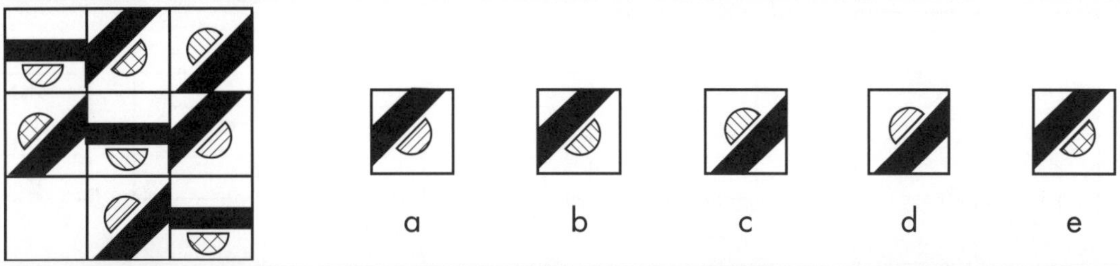

41

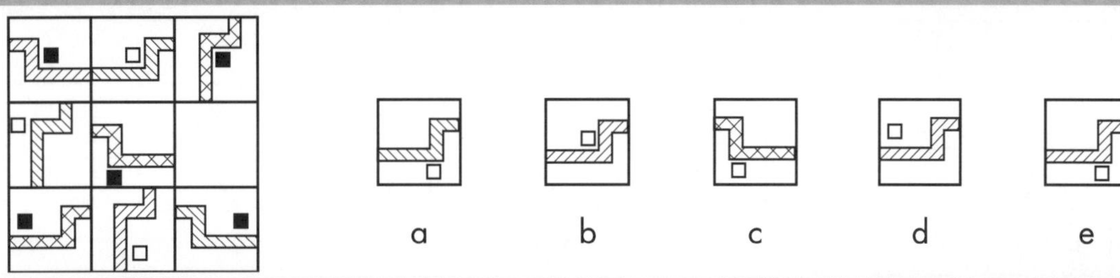

42

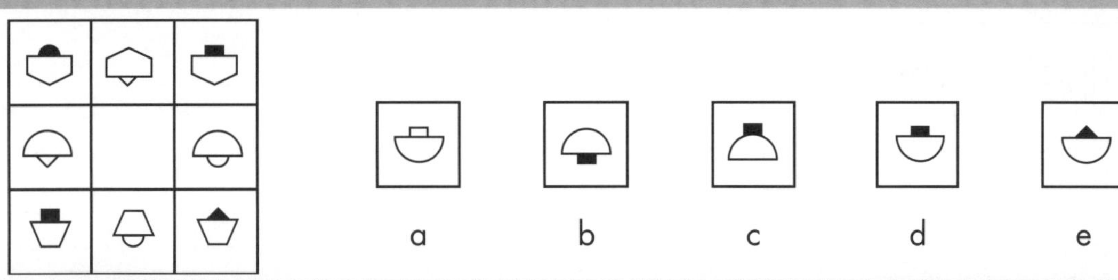

43

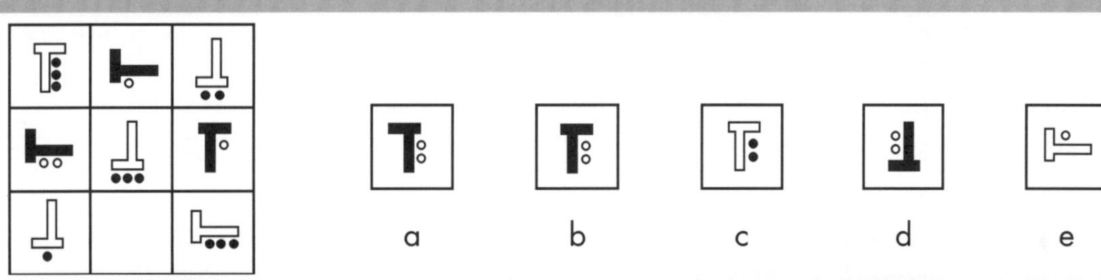

44

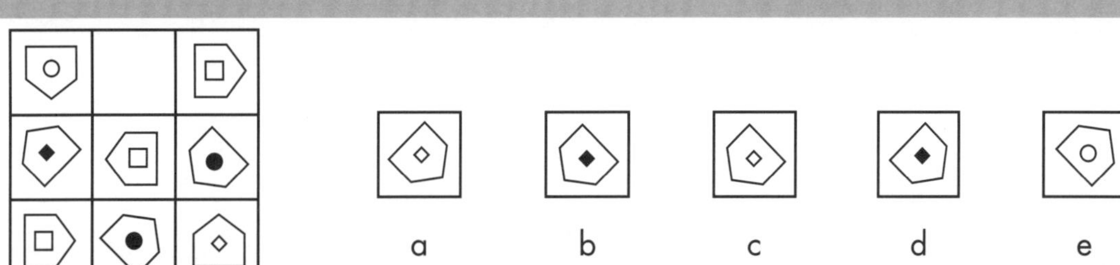

45

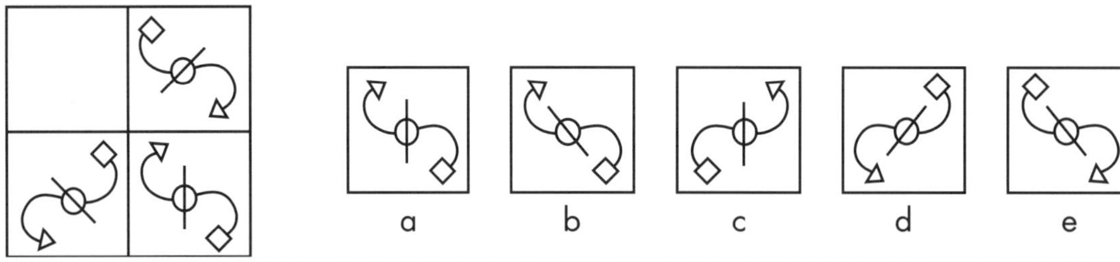

46

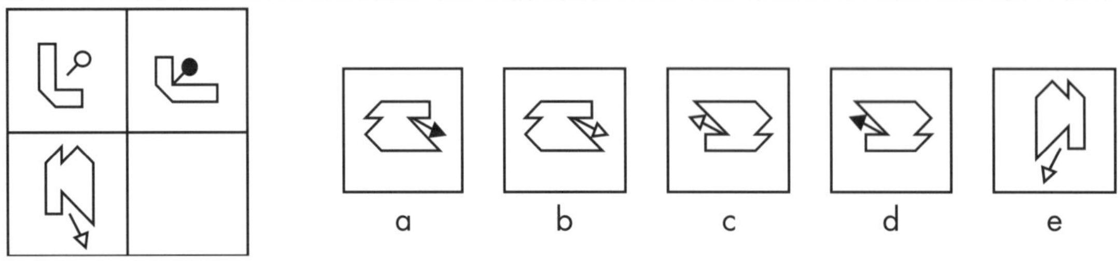

47

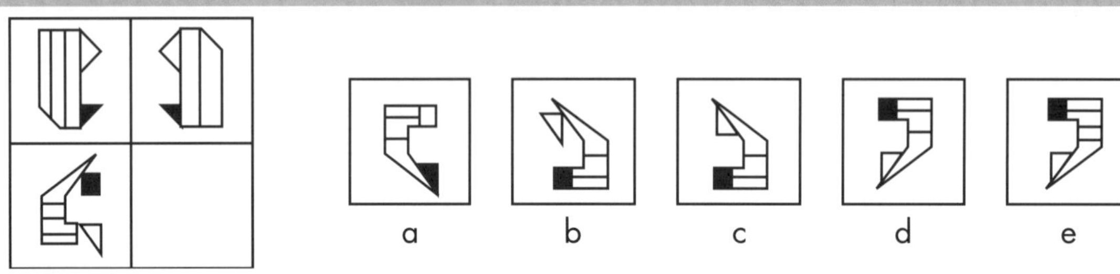

48

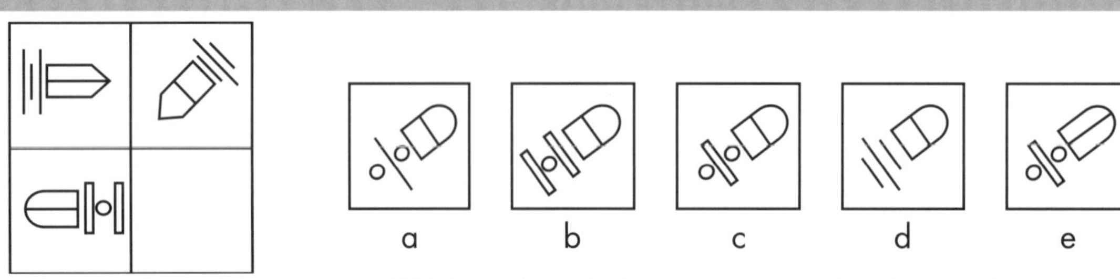

49

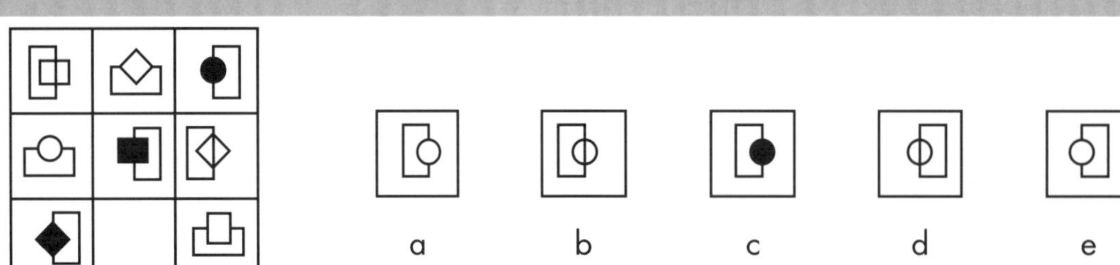

50

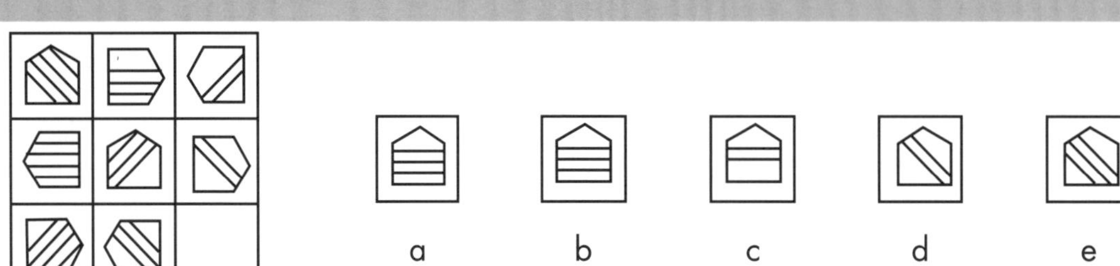

51

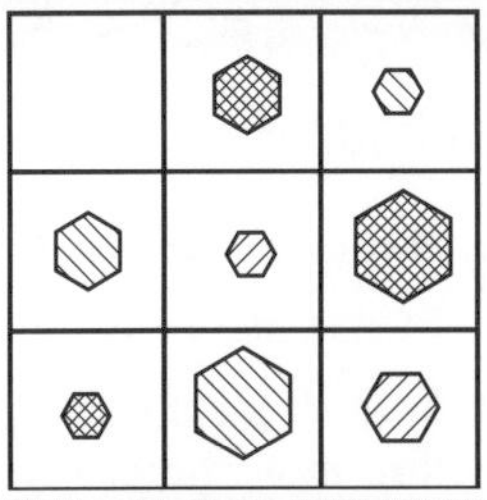

a b c d e

52

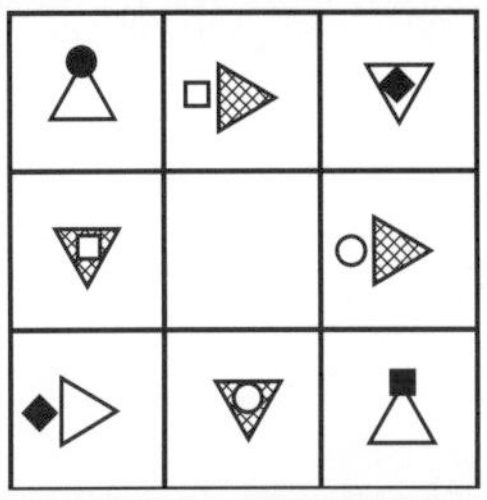

a b c d e

53

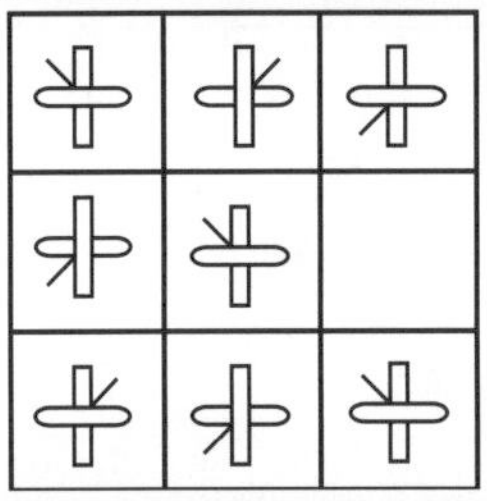

a b c d e

54

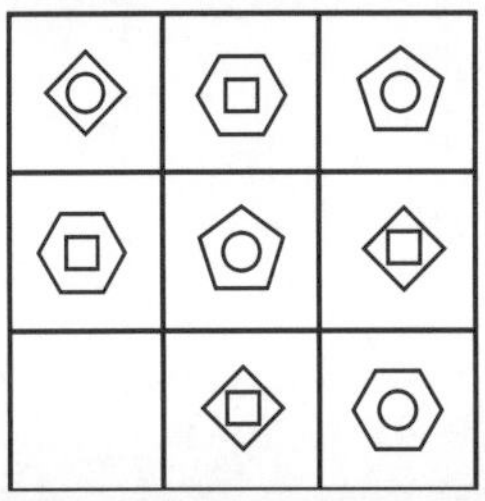

a b c d e

END OF SECTION

TYPE 2

In each question below, there are five shapes.

Find the shape that has the **least in common** with the four other shapes and mark its letter on the multiple choice sheet.

EXAMPLE 1 EXPLANATION

1. All of the choices contain a large white triangle which is pointing to the right, except **d**.

2. The answer, therefore, must be **d** as it doesn't have a characteristic that the other four choices share.

EXAMPLE 1

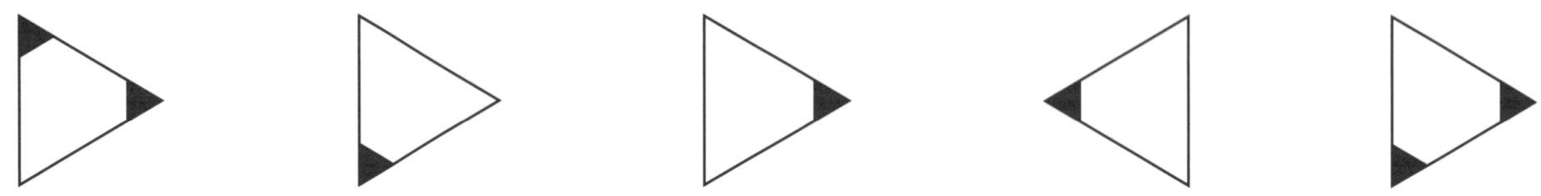

a b c **d** e

EXAMPLE 2

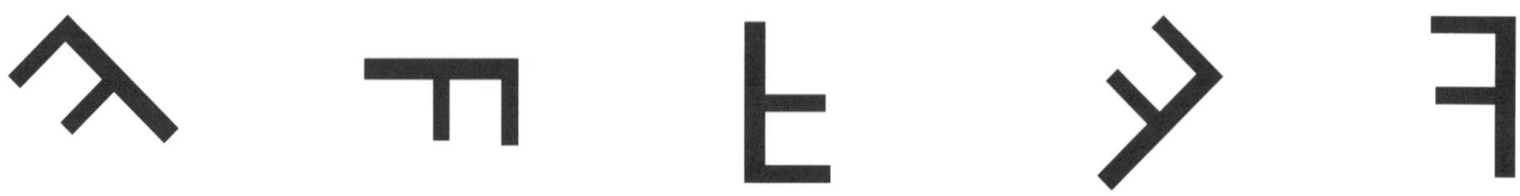

a **b** c d e

START OF SECTION

55

a b c d e

56

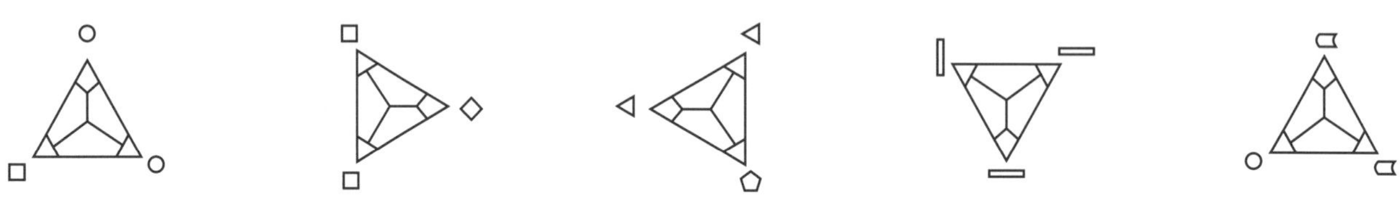

a b c d e

57

a b c d e

58

a b c d e

59

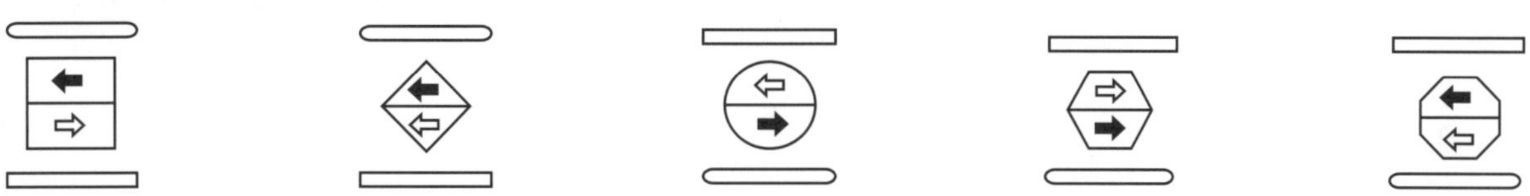

a b c d e

60

a b c d e

61

a b c d e

62

a b c d e

63

a b c d e

64

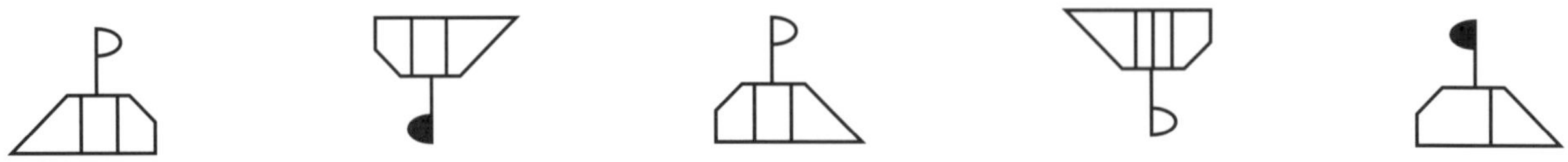

a b c d e

65

a b c d e

66

a b c d e

67

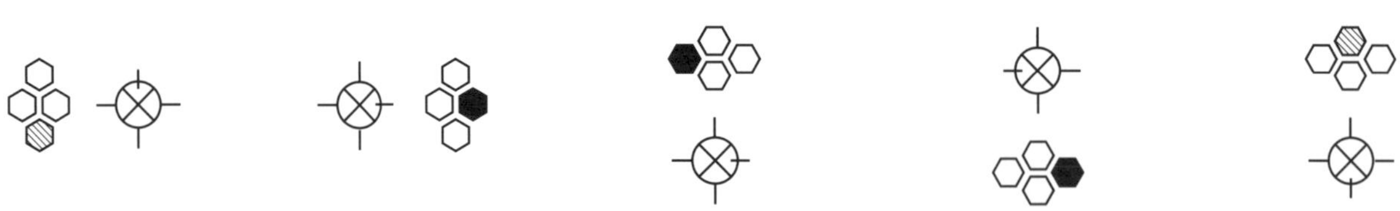

a b c d e

68

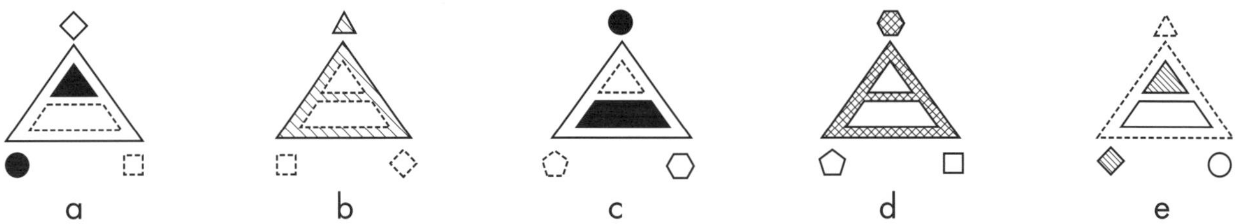

a b c d e

69

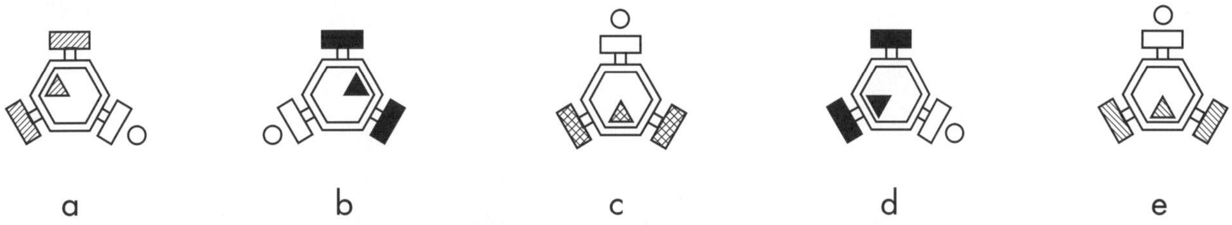

70

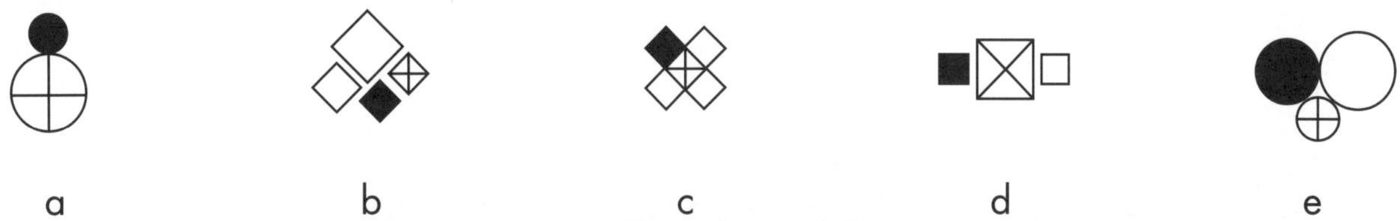

71

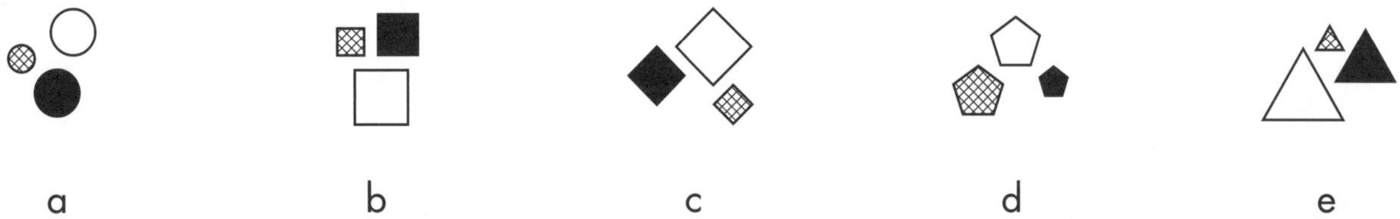

72

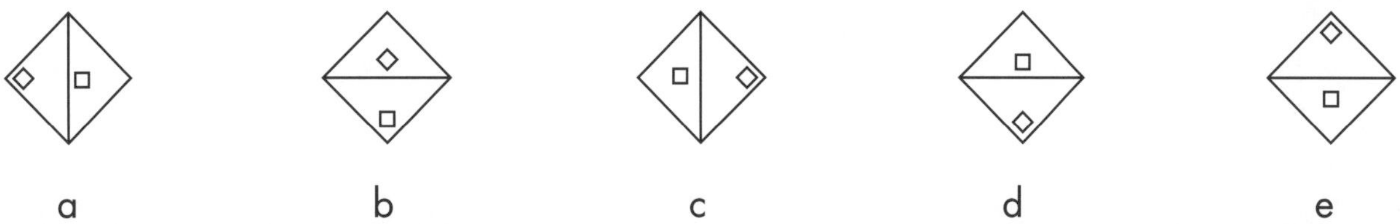

END OF TEST

[THIS PAGE IS INTENTIONALLY LEFT BLANK]

[THIS PAGE IS INTENTIONALLY LEFT BLANK]

NON VERBAL
TEST 12

Read the following instructions carefully:

1. Do not open this question booklet until you are instructed to do so.
2. This test has four sections, each containing 18 questions. There are 72 questions in total.
3. All your answers must be marked on the separate multiple choice sheet. Answers written on this question booklet will not be counted.
4. You may write any rough working on this question booklet.
5. For all questions you must select only one answer.
6. To mark your answer, draw a horizontal line through the rectangle next to your answer on the multiple choice sheet. If you want to change your answer, rub it out as completely as you can and then select your new answer.
7. Make sure you do not lose your place on the multiple choice sheet. Check that your answer box has the same number as the question that you are on.
8. You may not get to the end of the paper, but complete as many questions as you can. If a question is taking you too long, make sure you do not waste time on it and move forward to the next question. If you cannot decide which is the correct answer, select the one you think is most likely to be correct.
9. You have 50 minutes to complete this test. Work as quickly and carefully as you can.

Authors: Steven Vu and Graham Wildash

Published by Test Teach Limited.
Unit 203 Kingspark Business Centre, 152-178 Kingston Road, Kingston Upon Thames, KT3 3ST.

Test Teach

DO NOT OPEN THIS BOOKLET UNTIL TOLD TO DO SO

TYPE 4

In each question below, the shapes to the left of the vertical line are similar in a number of ways.

Select the shape from the five provided on the right which is the **most similar** to the shapes on the left.

Mark your answer on the multiple choice sheet.

EXAMPLE 1 EXPLANATION

1. Both shapes to the left of the black line contain a white rectangle. Therefore, the answer cannot be **b** as it does not contain a white rectangle, but instead has a square.

2. Both shapes to the left of black line also contain a black diamond. Therefore, the answer is **d**, as it is the only choice containing both a black diamond and a white rectangle.

EXAMPLE 1

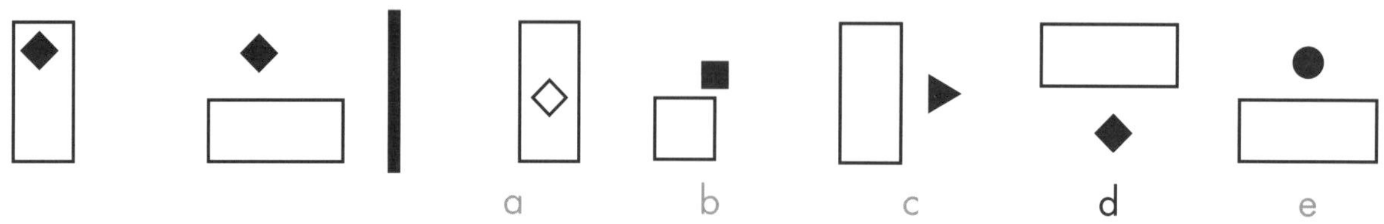

EXAMPLE 2

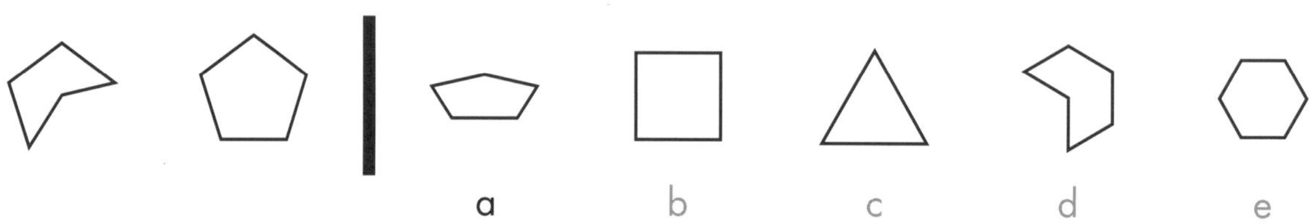

START OF SECTION

1

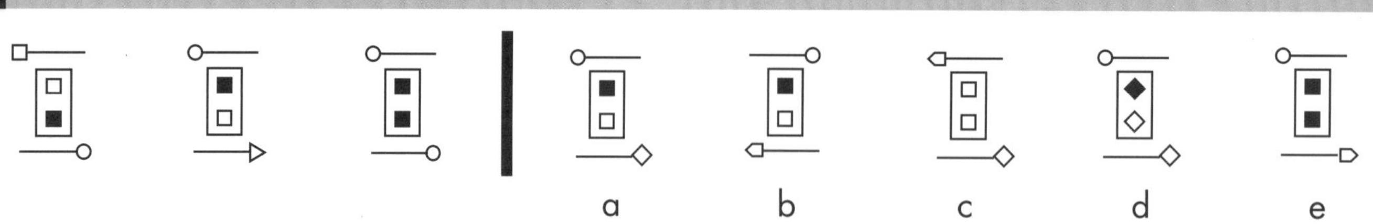

2

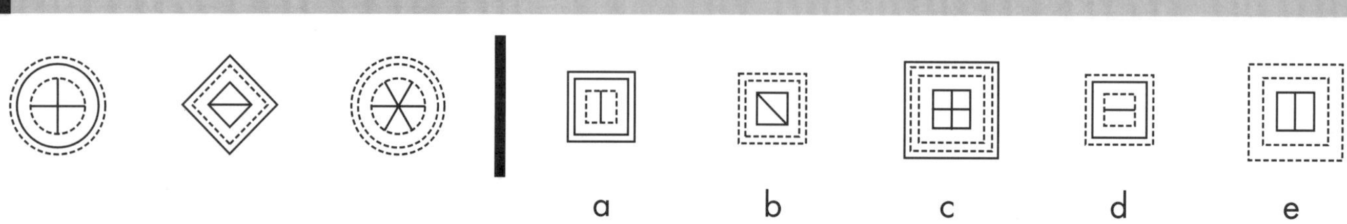

3

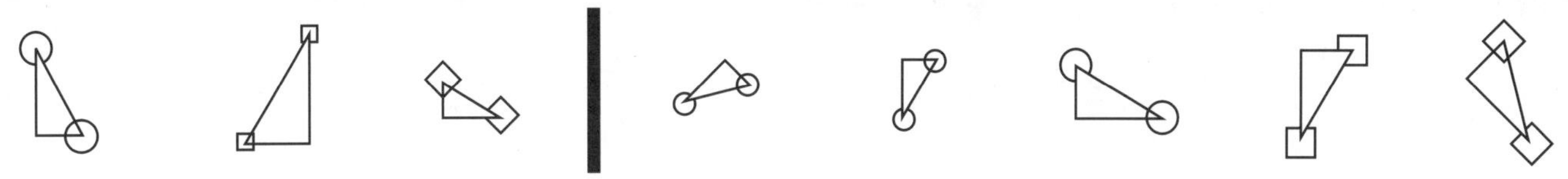

a b c d e

4

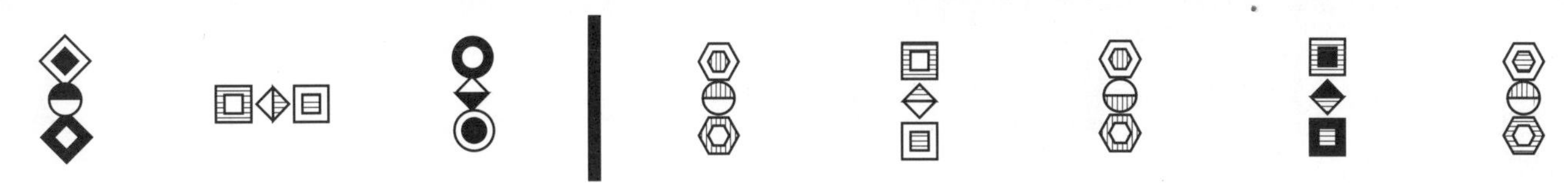

a b c d e

5

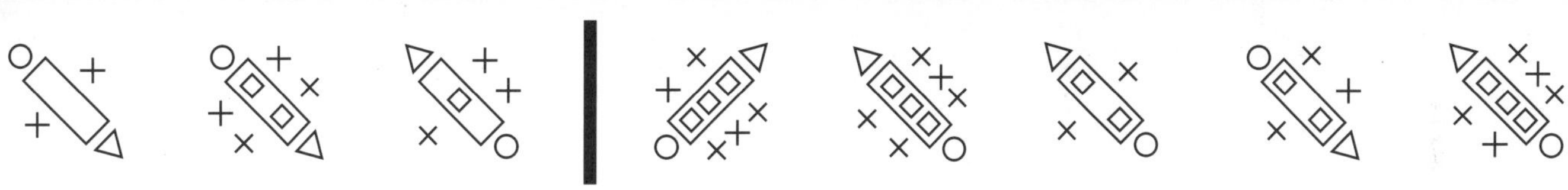

a b c d e

6

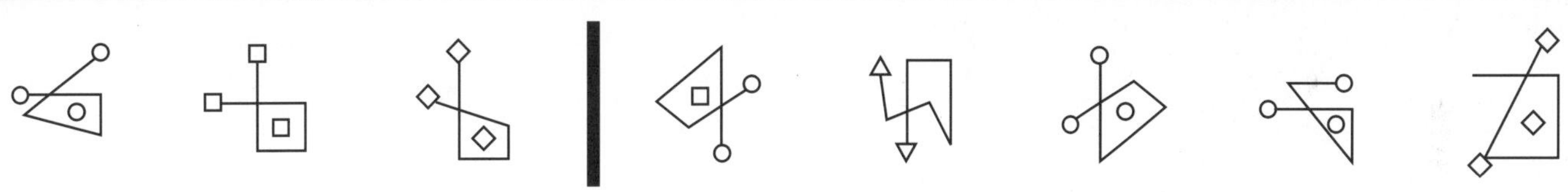

a b c d e

7

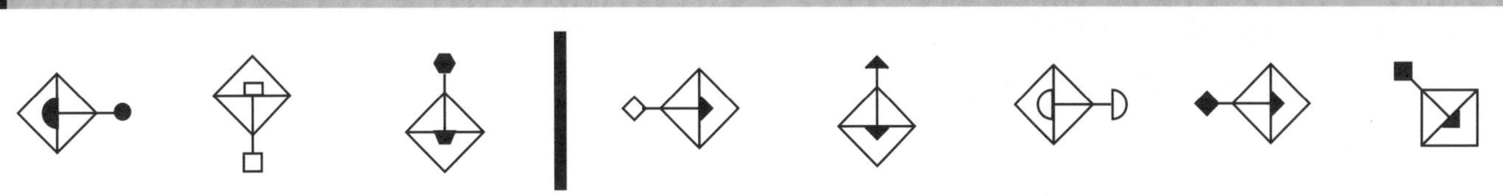

a b c d e

8

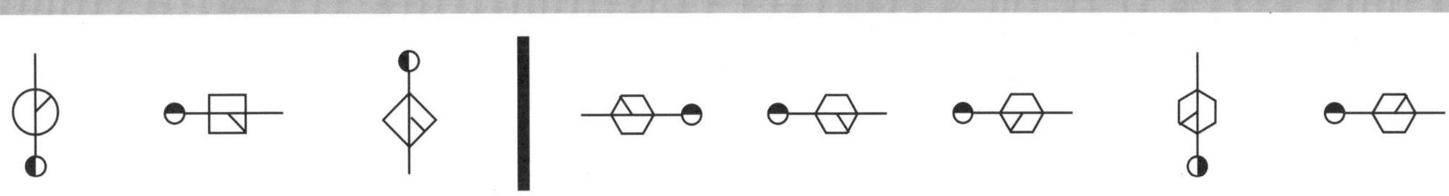

a b c d e

9

a b c d e

10

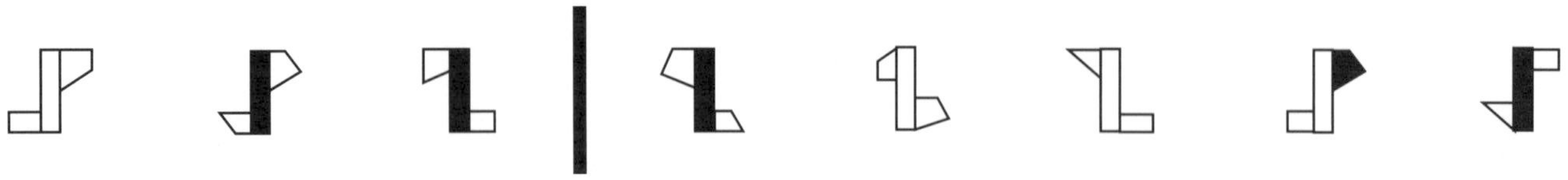

a b c d e

11

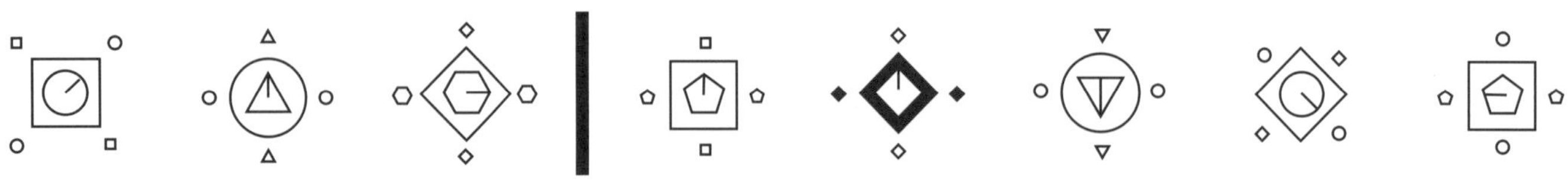

a b c d e

12

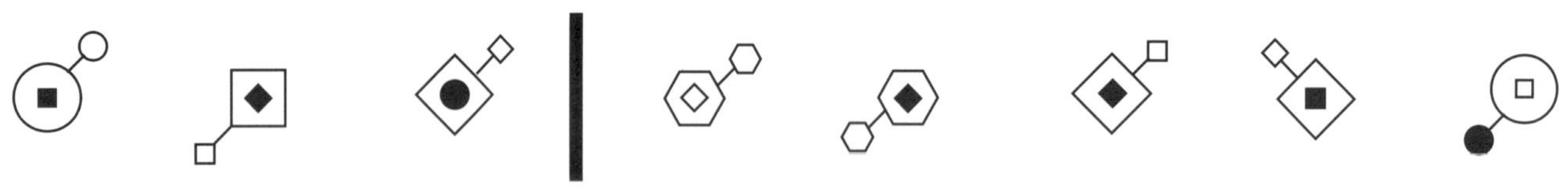

a b c d e

13

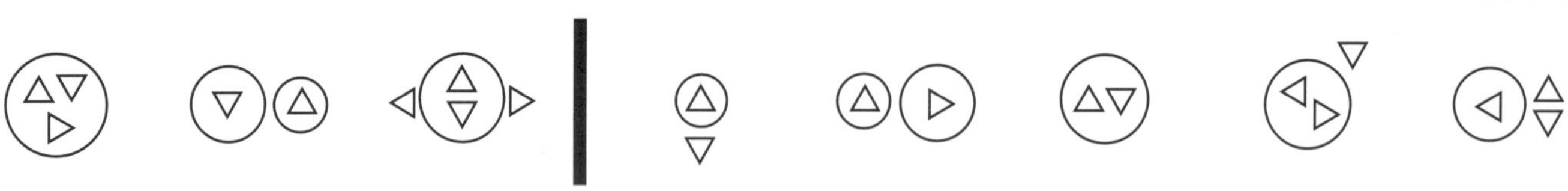

a b c d e

14

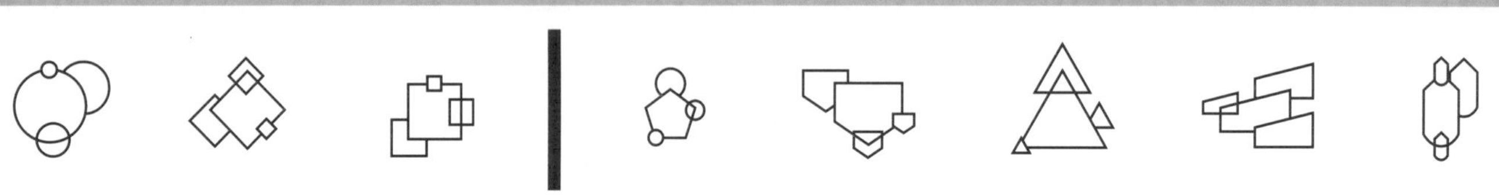

a b c d e

15

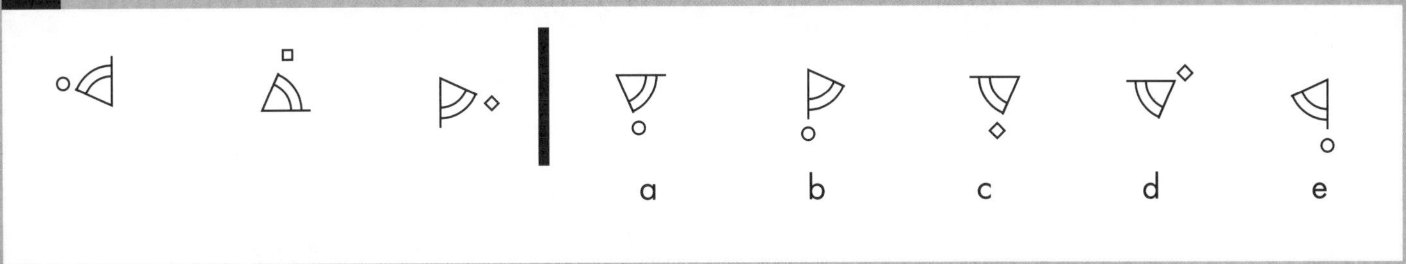

16

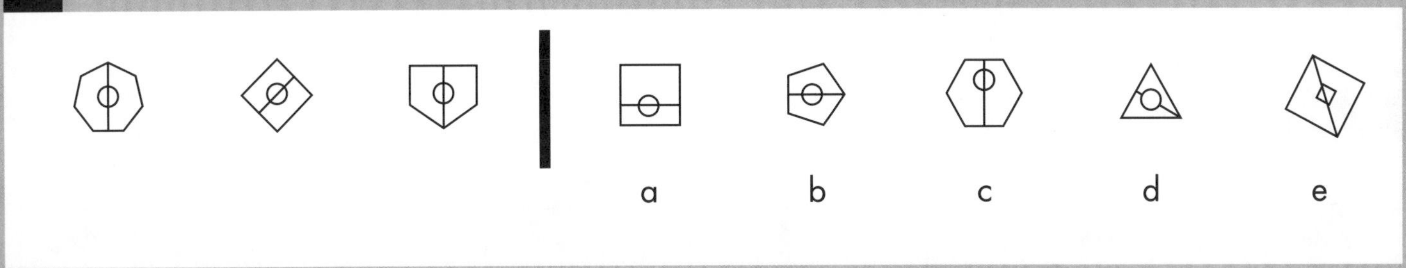

17

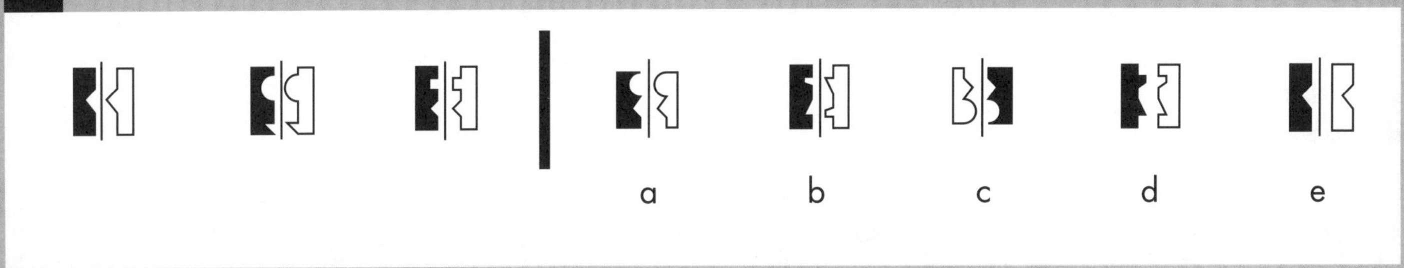

18

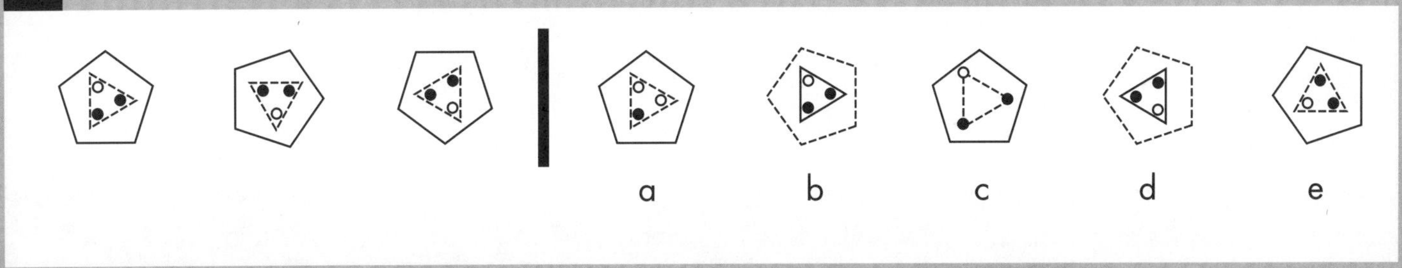

END OF SECTION

TYPE 7

In each question, five boxes have been **arranged in a sequence**. One box has been removed so that the sequence is no longer complete.

From the five options on the right, **find which box has been removed** and mark its letter on your multiple choice sheet.

EXAMPLE 1 EXPLANATION

1. The central shape is alternating in colour and shape. Our missing box, therefore, must contain a central shape which is a black square.

2. There is a small black square located in one of the corners in each box. It moves clockwise from corner to corner. Therefore, our missing box must also contain a small black square in its top left corner.

EXAMPLE 1

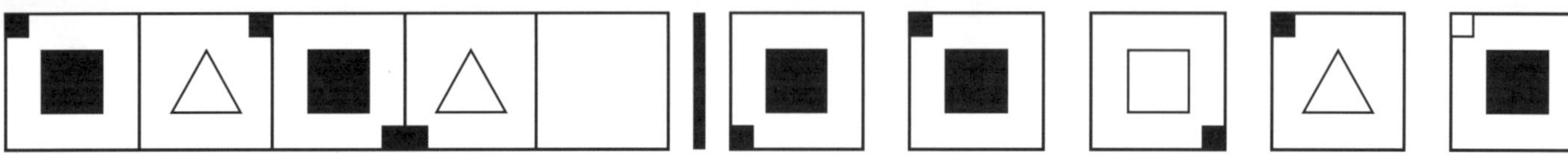

a b c d e

EXAMPLE 2

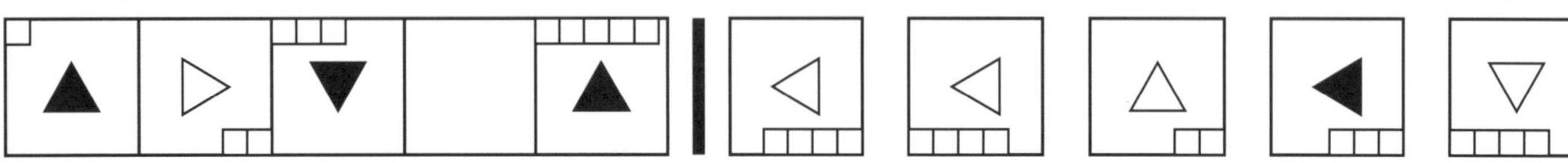

a b c d e

START OF SECTION

19

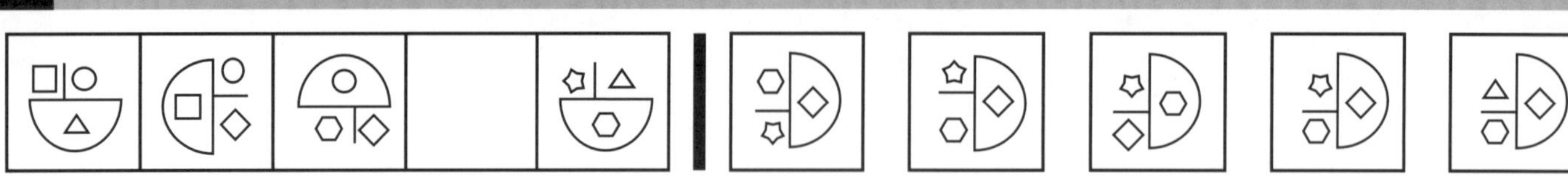

a b c d e

20

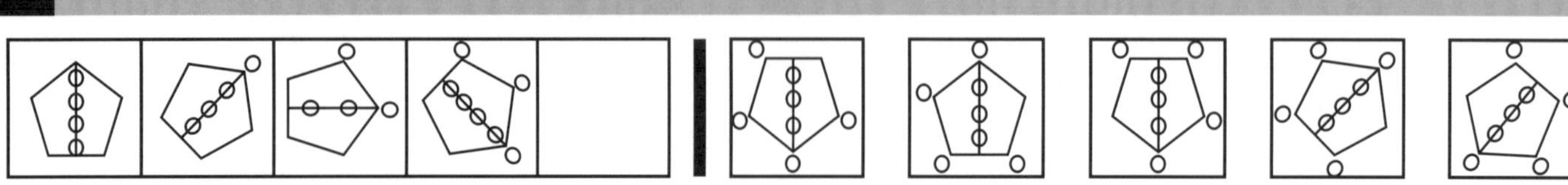

a b c d e

21

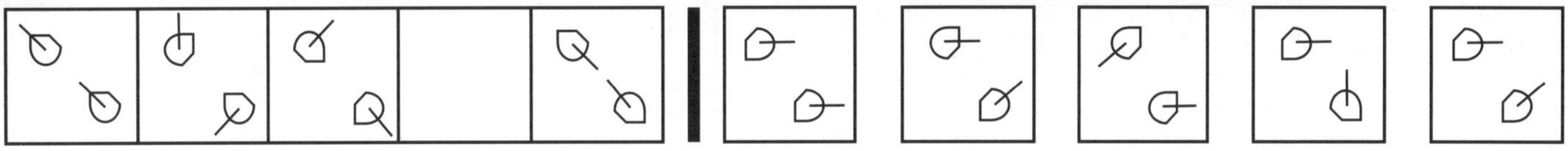

a b c d e

22

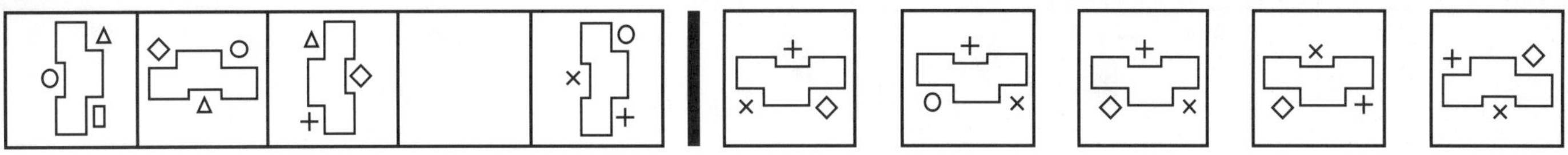

a b c d e

23

a b c d e

24

a b c d e

25

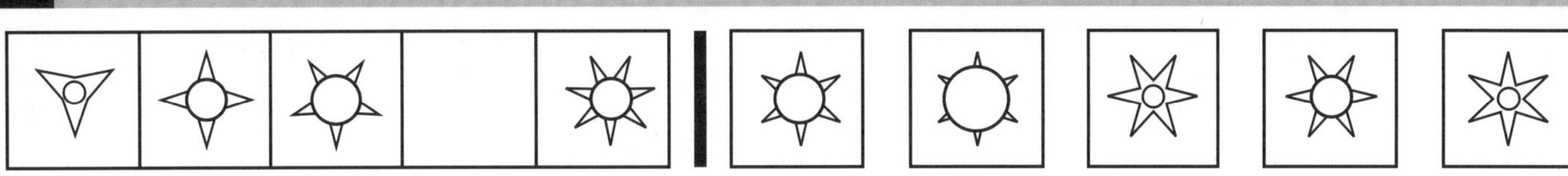

a b c d e

26

a b c d e

27

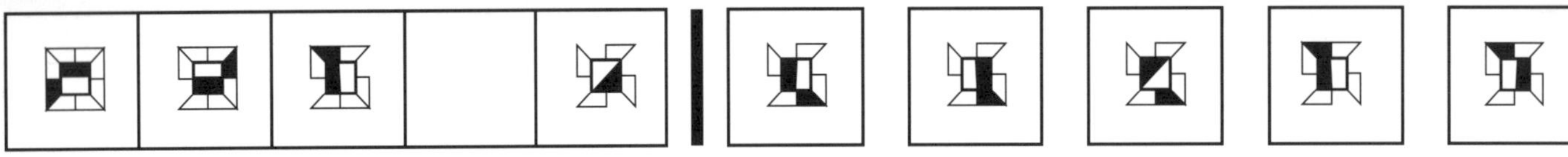

a b c d e

28

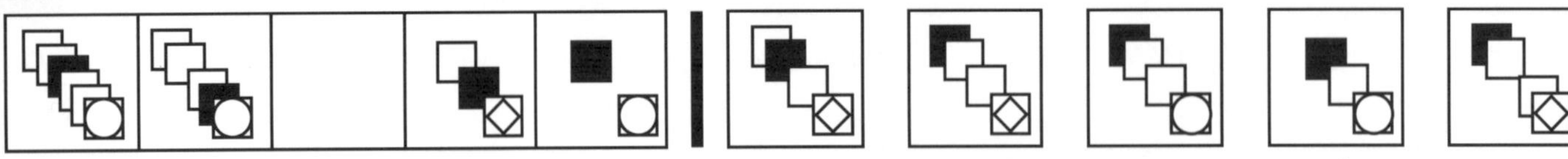

a b c d e

29

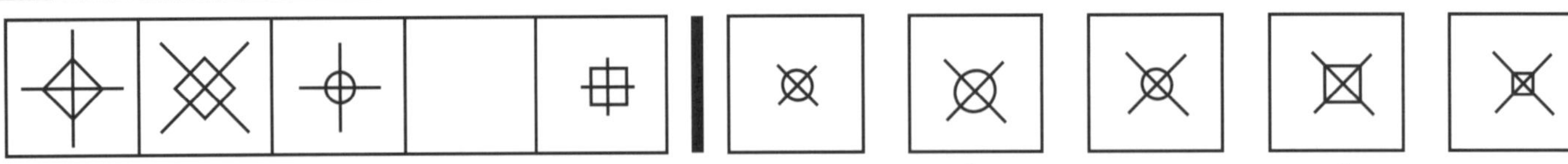

a b c d e

30

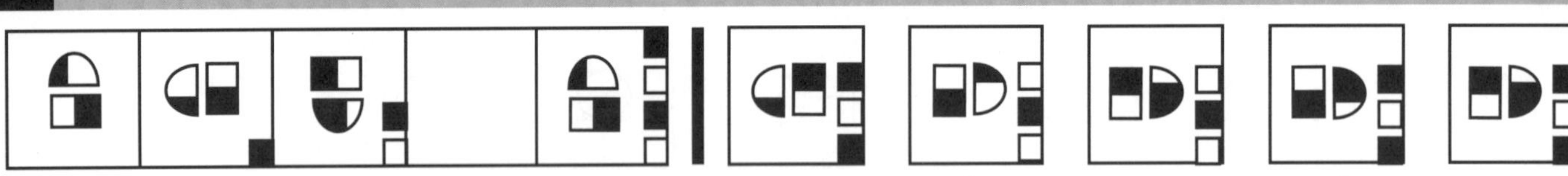

a b c d e

31

a b c d e

32

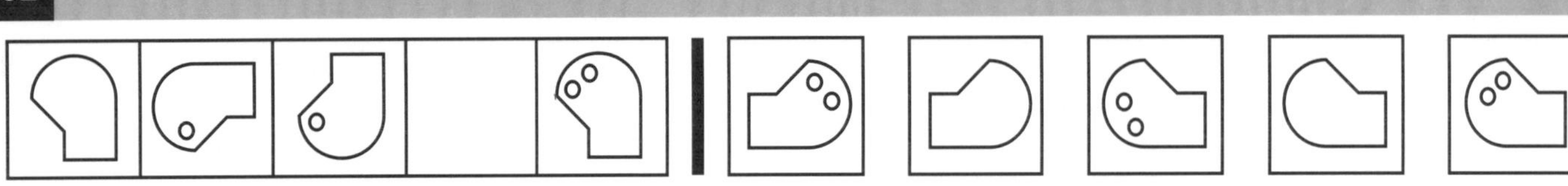

a b c d e

33

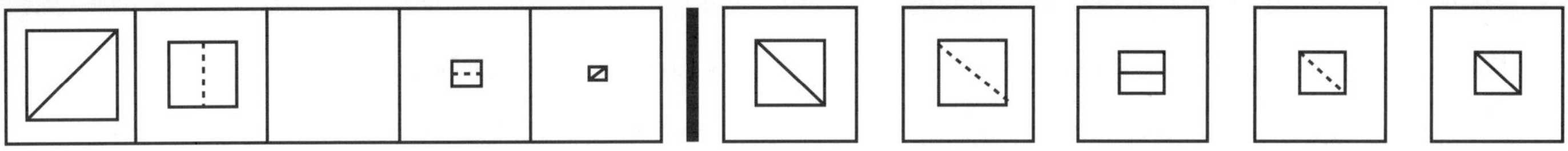

a b c d e

34

a b c d e

35

a b c d e

36

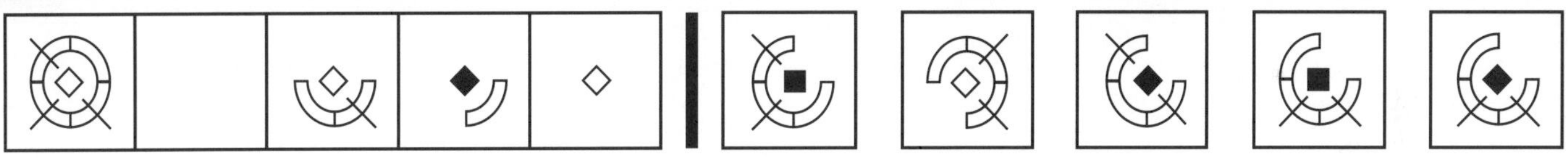

a b c d e

END OF SECTION

TYPE 6

In each question below, there are four boxes that have been identified with a two-letter code. The **top letters represent one characteristic** of the shapes contained within the boxes, the **bottom letters represent another**.

By working out what the letters represent, you must select the correct two-letter code to **describe the shape** found in the box to the right of the black line.

Mark your answer on the multiple choice sheet.

EXAMPLE 1 EXPLANATION

1. Boxes one and three share the same top letter and also contain shapes which are black. The top letter, therefore, represents the shading of the shape. Our shape is striped vertically, the same as the second shape, so its top letter must be E.

2. Boxes three and four share the same bottom letter and both contain shapes that point upwards. Our shape also points upwards, so the bottom letter of our box is C.

EXAMPLE 1

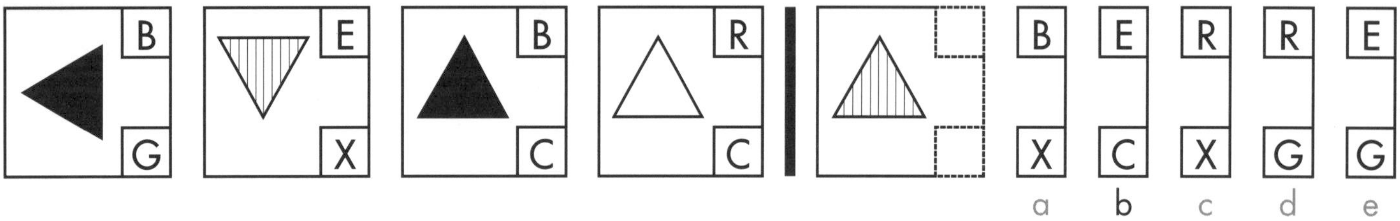

EXAMPLE 2

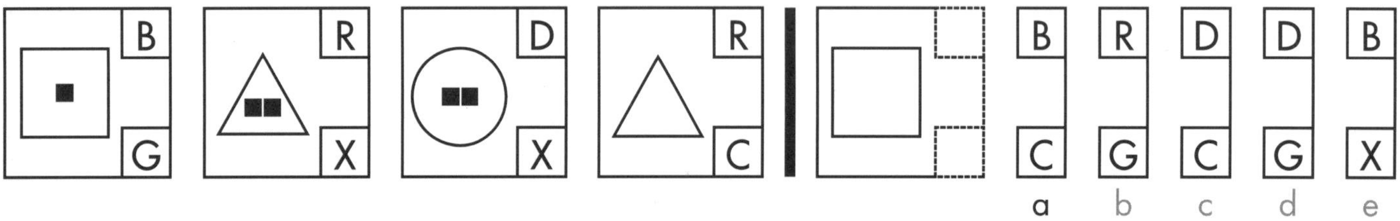

START OF SECTION

37

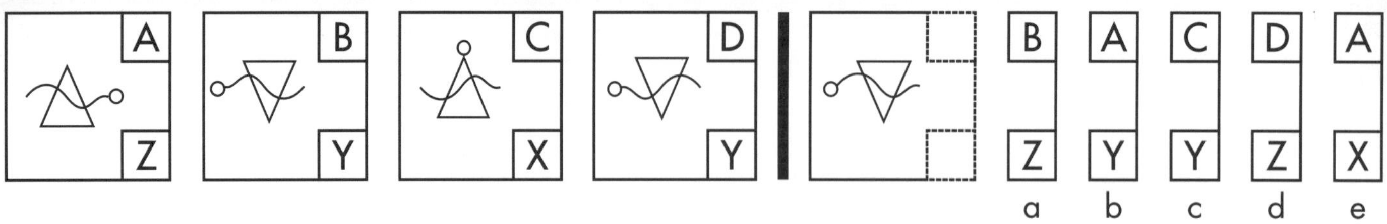

38

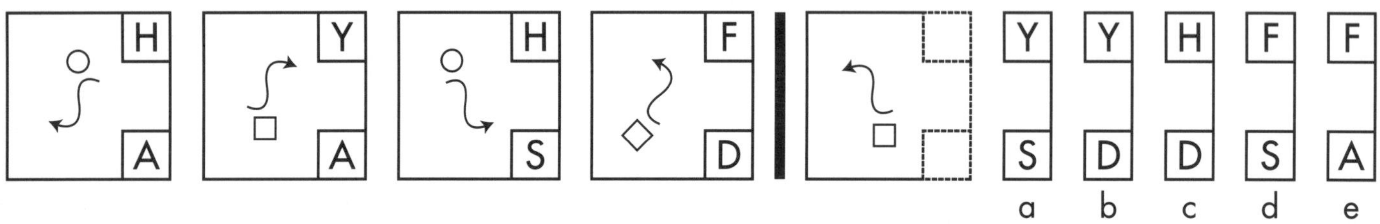

39

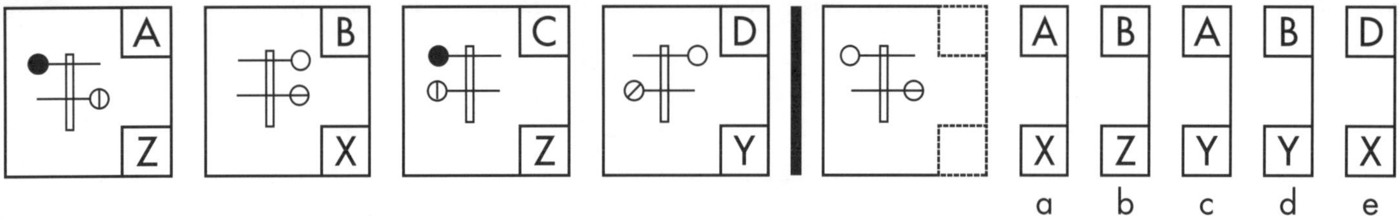

40

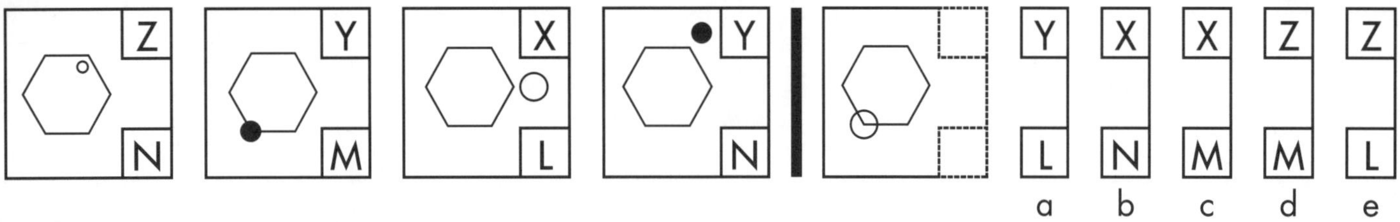

41

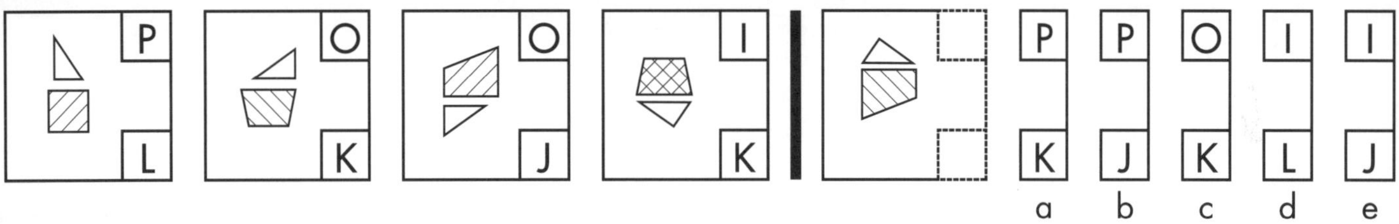

42

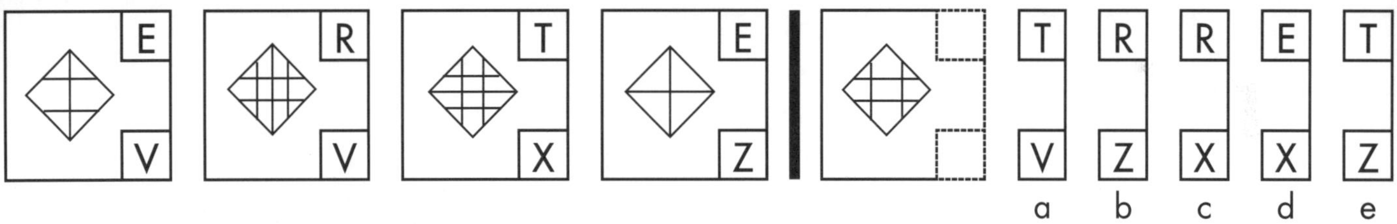

43

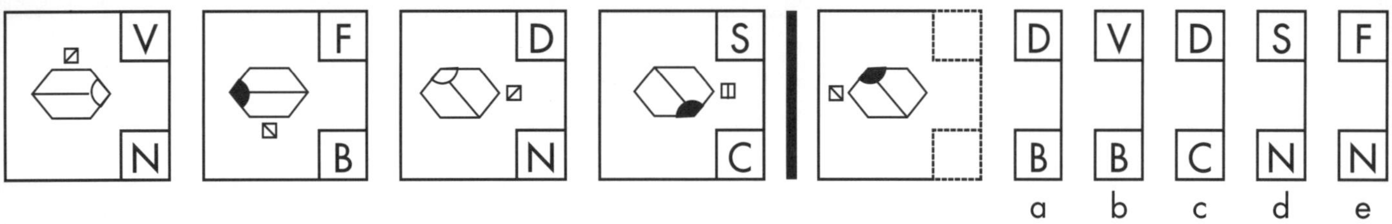

44

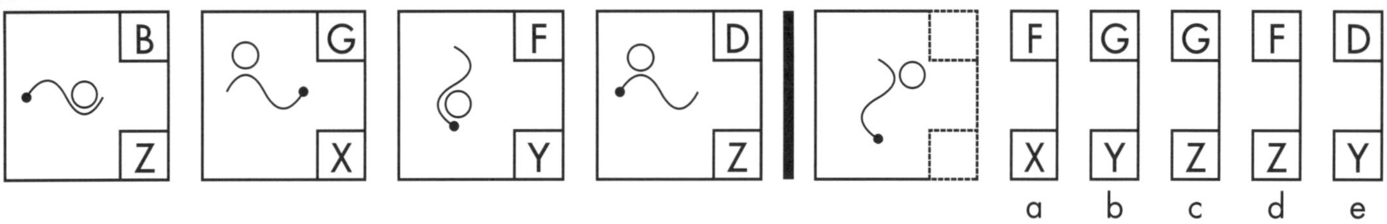

45

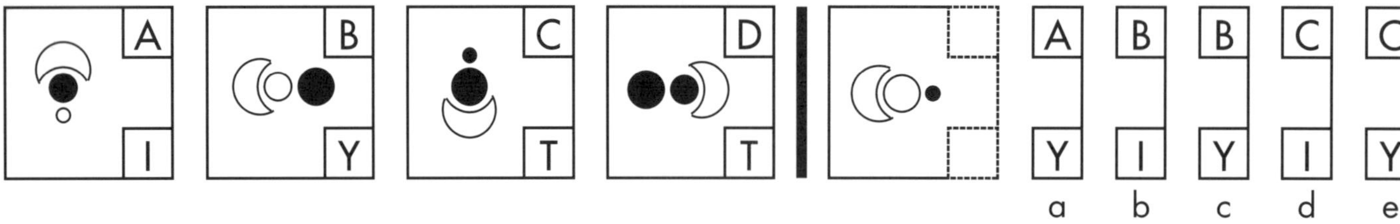

46

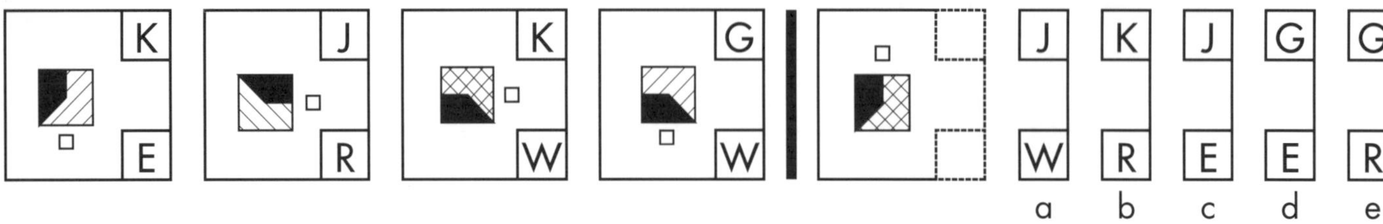

47

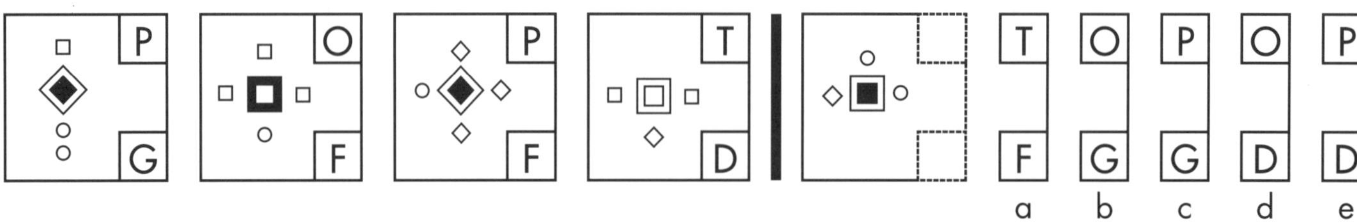

48

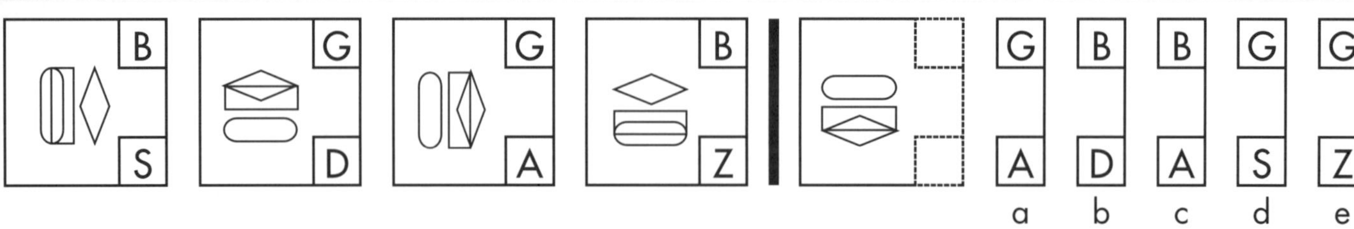

49

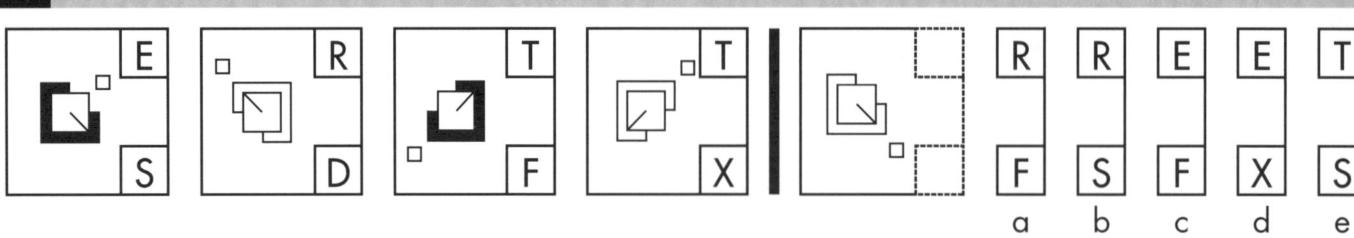

50

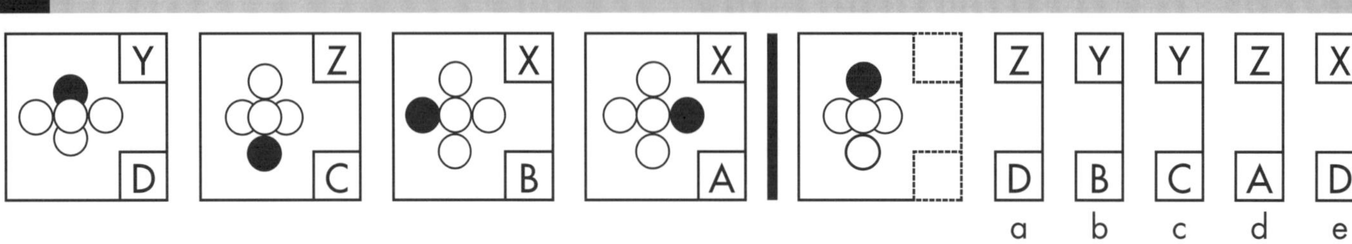

51

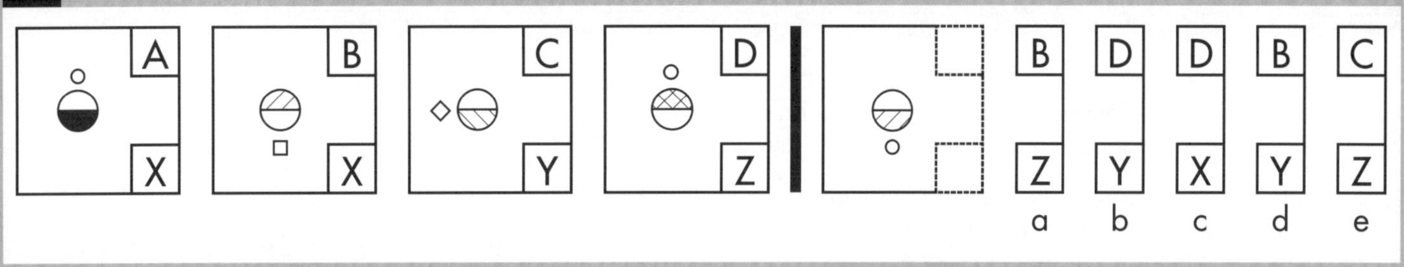

52

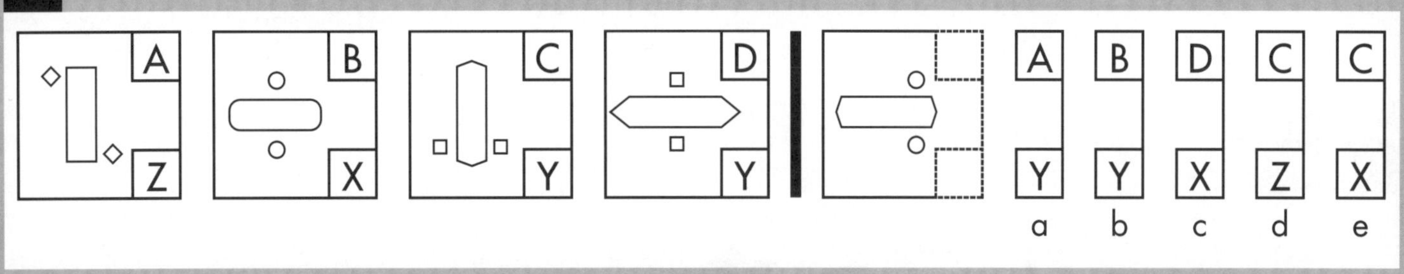

53

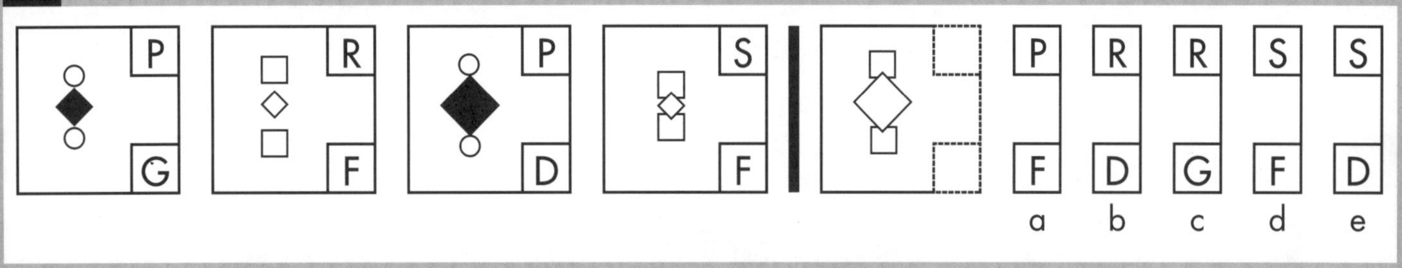

54

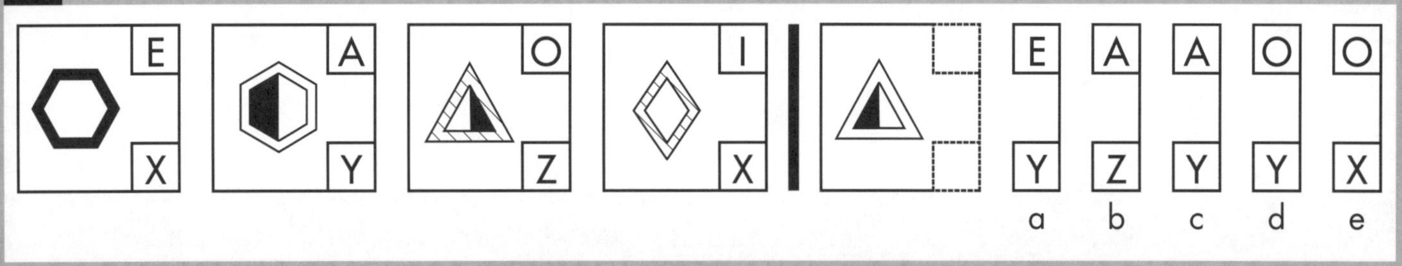

END OF SECTION

TYPE 3

In each question below, there are two shapes on the left hand side which are **related to each other**. To the right of the dots there is a third shape.

Pick a fourth shape from the five available options so that the third and fourth shape **share the same relationship** as the first and second shape.

Mark your choice on the multiple choice sheet.

EXAMPLE 1 EXPLANATION

1. In the first pair of shapes, the colour changes from white to black. Therefore, the shading of our shape, which is a white hexagon, must also change to black.

2. In the first pair of shapes, the first shape rotates 45° to give the second shape. Therefore, our shape must also rotate 45°.

3. In the first pair of shapes, the size of the first shape shrinks, therefore, our shape must become smaller.

EXAMPLE 1

a b c d e

EXAMPLE 2

a b c d e

START OF SECTION

55

a b c d e

56

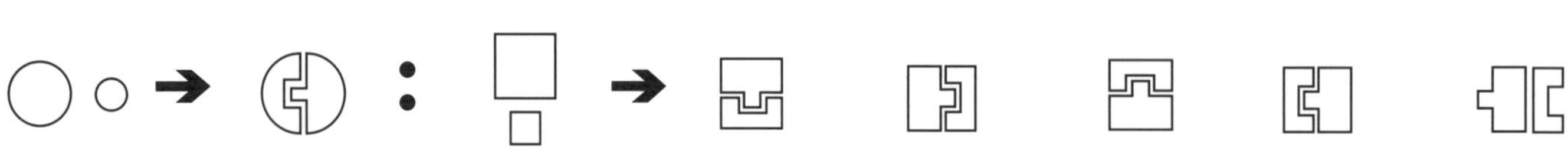

a b c d e

57

a b c d e

58

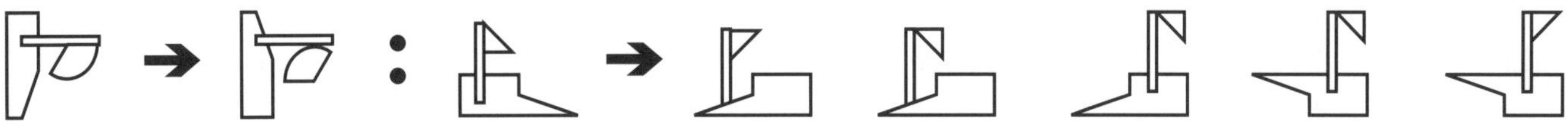

a b c d e

59

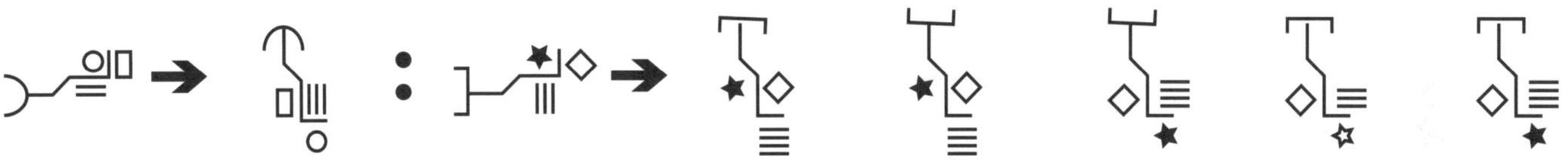

a b c d e

60

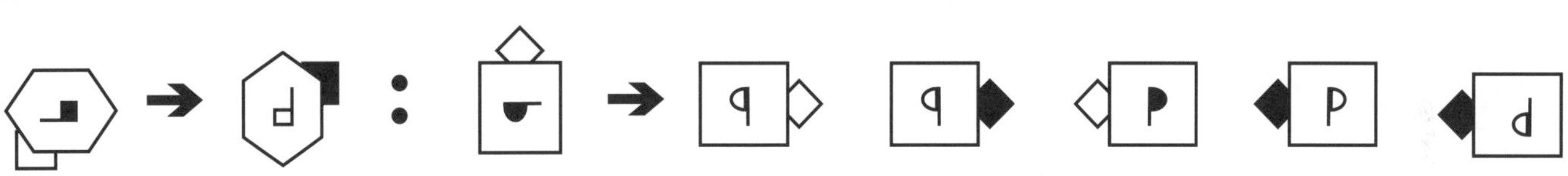

a b c d e

61

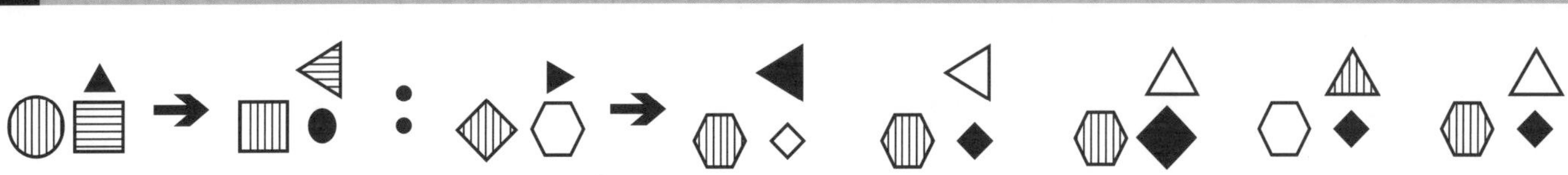

a b c d e

62

a b c d e

63

a b c d e

64

a b c d e

65

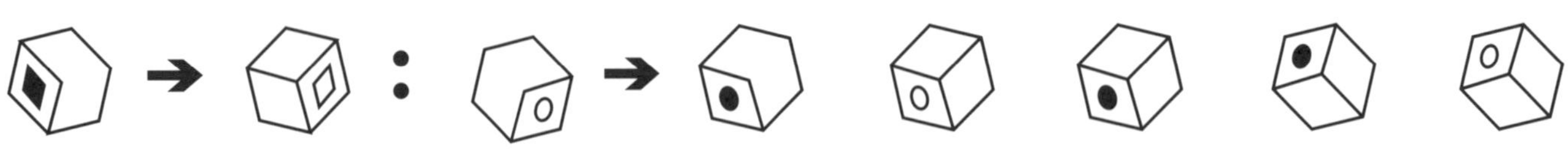

a b c d e

66

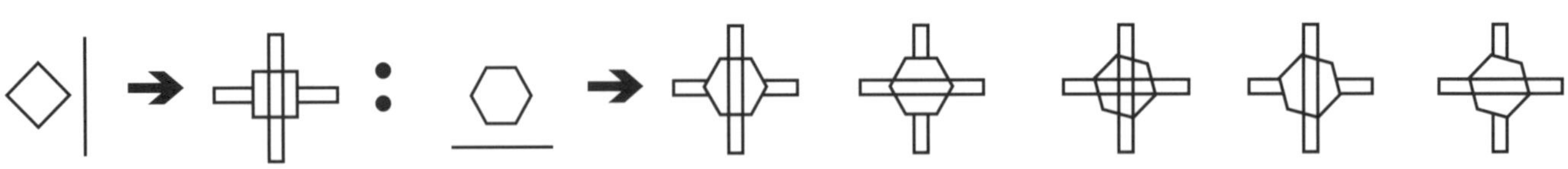

a b c d e

67

a b c d e

68

a b c d e

69

a b c d e

70

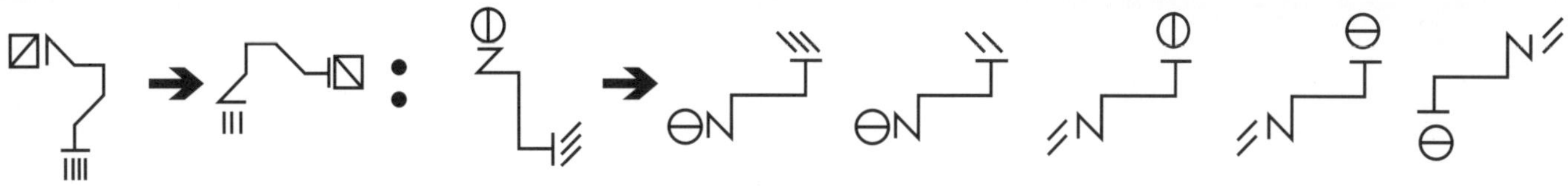

a b c d e

71

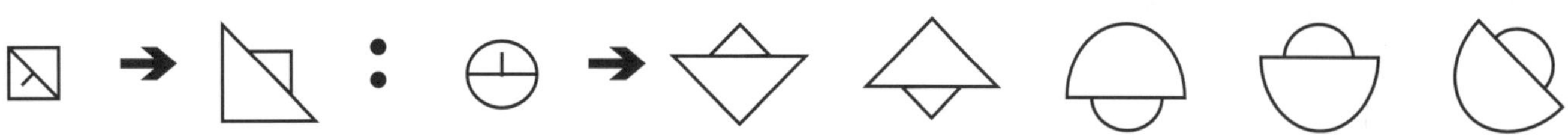

a b c d e

72

a b c d e

END OF TEST

[THIS PAGE IS INTENTIONALLY LEFT BLANK]

[THIS PAGE IS INTENTIONALLY LEFT BLANK]

41	A	B	C	D	E
42	A	B	C	D	E
43	A	B	C	D	E
44	A	B	C	D	E
45	A	B	C	D	E
46	A	B	C	D	E
47	A	B	C	D	E
48	A	B	C	D	E
49	A	B	C	D	E
50	A	B	C	D	E
51	A	B	C	D	E
52	A	B	C	D	E
53	A	B	C	D	E
54	A	B	C	D	E
55	A	B	C	D	E
56	A	B	C	D	E
57	A	B	C	D	E
58	A	B	C	D	E
59	A	B	C	D	E
60	A	B	C	D	E
61	A	B	C	D	E
62	A	B	C	D	E
63	A	B	C	D	E
64	A	B	C	D	E
65	A	B	C	D	E
66	A	B	C	D	E
67	A	B	C	D	E
68	A	B	C	D	E
69	A	B	C	D	E
70	A	B	C	D	E
71	A	B	C	D	E
72	A	B	C	D	E

Test Teach

NON VERBAL
TEST 12

MULTIPLE CHOICE

NAME

DATE OF BIRTH

SCORE

1 A B C D E

2 A B C D E

3 A B C D E

4 A B C D E

5 A B C D E

6 A B C D E

7 A B C D E

8 A B C D E

9 A B C D E

10 A B C D E

11 A B C D E

12 A B C D E

13 A B C D E

14 A B C D E

15 A B C D E

16 A B C D E

17 A B C D E

18 A B C D E

19 A B C D E

20 A B C D E

21 A B C D E

22 A B C D E

23 A B C D E

24 A B C D E

25 A B C D E

26 A B C D E

27 A B C D E

28 A B C D E

29 A B C D E

30 A B C D E

31 A B C D E

32 A B C D E

33 A B C D E

34 A B C D E

35 A B C D E

36 A B C D E

37 A B C D E

38 A B C D E

39 A B C D E

40 A B C D E

41	42	43	44	45	46	47	48
A ☐	A ☐	A ☐	A ☐	A ☐	A ☐	A ☐	A ☐
B ☐	B ☐	B ☐	B ☐	B ☐	B ☐	B ☐	B ☐
C ☐	C ☐	C ☐	C ☐	C ☐	C ☐	C ☐	C ☐
D ☐	D ☐	D ☐	D ☐	D ☐	D ☐	D ☐	D ☐
E ☐	E ☐	E ☐	E ☐	E ☐	E ☐	E ☐	E ☐

49	50	51	52	53	54	55	56
A ☐	A ☐	A ☐	A ☐	A ☐	A ☐	A ☐	A ☐
B ☐	B ☐	B ☐	B ☐	B ☐	B ☐	B ☐	B ☐
C ☐	C ☐	C ☐	C ☐	C ☐	C ☐	C ☐	C ☐
D ☐	D ☐	D ☐	D ☐	D ☐	D ☐	D ☐	D ☐
E ☐	E ☐	E ☐	E ☐	E ☐	E ☐	E ☐	E ☐

57	58	59	60	61	62	63	64
A ☐	A ☐	A ☐	A ☐	A ☐	A ☐	A ☐	A ☐
B ☐	B ☐	B ☐	B ☐	B ☐	B ☐	B ☐	B ☐
C ☐	C ☐	C ☐	C ☐	C ☐	C ☐	C ☐	C ☐
D ☐	D ☐	D ☐	D ☐	D ☐	D ☐	D ☐	D ☐
E ☐	E ☐	E ☐	E ☐	E ☐	E ☐	E ☐	E ☐

65	66	67	68	69	70	71	72
A ☐	A ☐	A ☐	A ☐	A ☐	A ☐	A ☐	A ☐
B ☐	B ☐	B ☐	B ☐	B ☐	B ☐	B ☐	B ☐
C ☐	C ☐	C ☐	C ☐	C ☐	C ☐	C ☐	C ☐
D ☐	D ☐	D ☐	D ☐	D ☐	D ☐	D ☐	D ☐
E ☐	E ☐	E ☐	E ☐	E ☐	E ☐	E ☐	E ☐

NON VERBAL
TEST 11

MULTIPLE CHOICE

NAME

DATE OF BIRTH

SCORE

Question					
1	A ☐	B ☐	C ☐	D ☐	E ☐
2	A ☐	B ☐	C ☐	D ☐	E ☐
3	A ☐	B ☐	C ☐	D ☐	E ☐
4	A ☐	B ☐	C ☐	D ☐	E ☐
5	A ☐	B ☐	C ☐	D ☐	E ☐
6	A ☐	B ☐	C ☐	D ☐	E ☐
7	A ☐	B ☐	C ☐	D ☐	E ☐
8	A ☐	B ☐	C ☐	D ☐	E ☐
9	A ☐	B ☐	C ☐	D ☐	E ☐
10	A ☐	B ☐	C ☐	D ☐	E ☐
11	A ☐	B ☐	C ☐	D ☐	E ☐
12	A ☐	B ☐	C ☐	D ☐	E ☐
13	A ☐	B ☐	C ☐	D ☐	E ☐
14	A ☐	B ☐	C ☐	D ☐	E ☐
15	A ☐	B ☐	C ☐	D ☐	E ☐
16	A ☐	B ☐	C ☐	D ☐	E ☐
17	A ☐	B ☐	C ☐	D ☐	E ☐
18	A ☐	B ☐	C ☐	D ☐	E ☐
19	A ☐	B ☐	C ☐	D ☐	E ☐
20	A ☐	B ☐	C ☐	D ☐	E ☐
21	A ☐	B ☐	C ☐	D ☐	E ☐
22	A ☐	B ☐	C ☐	D ☐	E ☐
23	A ☐	B ☐	C ☐	D ☐	E ☐
24	A ☐	B ☐	C ☐	D ☐	E ☐
25	A ☐	B ☐	C ☐	D ☐	E ☐
26	A ☐	B ☐	C ☐	D ☐	E ☐
27	A ☐	B ☐	C ☐	D ☐	E ☐
28	A ☐	B ☐	C ☐	D ☐	E ☐
29	A ☐	B ☐	C ☐	D ☐	E ☐
30	A ☐	B ☐	C ☐	D ☐	E ☐
31	A ☐	B ☐	C ☐	D ☐	E ☐
32	A ☐	B ☐	C ☐	D ☐	E ☐
33	A ☐	B ☐	C ☐	D ☐	E ☐
34	A ☐	B ☐	C ☐	D ☐	E ☐
35	A ☐	B ☐	C ☐	D ☐	E ☐
36	A ☐	B ☐	C ☐	D ☐	E ☐
37	A ☐	B ☐	C ☐	D ☐	E ☐
38	A ☐	B ☐	C ☐	D ☐	E ☐
39	A ☐	B ☐	C ☐	D ☐	E ☐
40	A ☐	B ☐	C ☐	D ☐	E ☐

41	42	43	44	45	46	47	48
A ☐	A ☐	A ☐	A ☐	A ☐	A ☐	A ☐	A ☐
B ☐	B ☐	B ☐	B ☐	B ☐	B ☐	B ☐	B ☐
C ☐	C ☐	C ☐	C ☐	C ☐	C ☐	C ☐	C ☐
D ☐	D ☐	D ☐	D ☐	D ☐	D ☐	D ☐	D ☐
E ☐	E ☐	E ☐	E ☐	E ☐	E ☐	E ☐	E ☐

49	50	51	52	53	54	55	56
A ☐	A ☐	A ☐	A ☐	A ☐	A ☐	A ☐	A ☐
B ☐	B ☐	B ☐	B ☐	B ☐	B ☐	B ☐	B ☐
C ☐	C ☐	C ☐	C ☐	C ☐	C ☐	C ☐	C ☐
D ☐	D ☐	D ☐	D ☐	D ☐	D ☐	D ☐	D ☐
E ☐	E ☐	E ☐	E ☐	E ☐	E ☐	E ☐	E ☐

57	58	59	60	61	62	63	64
A ☐	A ☐	A ☐	A ☐	A ☐	A ☐	A ☐	A ☐
B ☐	B ☐	B ☐	B ☐	B ☐	B ☐	B ☐	B ☐
C ☐	C ☐	C ☐	C ☐	C ☐	C ☐	C ☐	C ☐
D ☐	D ☐	D ☐	D ☐	D ☐	D ☐	D ☐	D ☐
E ☐	E ☐	E ☐	E ☐	E ☐	E ☐	E ☐	E ☐

65	66	67	68	69	70	71	72
A ☐	A ☐	A ☐	A ☐	A ☐	A ☐	A ☐	A ☐
B ☐	B ☐	B ☐	B ☐	B ☐	B ☐	B ☐	B ☐
C ☐	C ☐	C ☐	C ☐	C ☐	C ☐	C ☐	C ☐
D ☐	D ☐	D ☐	D ☐	D ☐	D ☐	D ☐	D ☐
E ☐	E ☐	E ☐	E ☐	E ☐	E ☐	E ☐	E ☐

Test Teach

NON VERBAL
TEST 10

MULTIPLE CHOICE

NAME

DATE OF BIRTH

SCORE

1	2	3	4	5	6	7	8
A ☐	A ☐	A ☐	A ☐	A ☐	A ☐	A ☐	A ☐
B ☐	B ☐	B ☐	B ☐	B ☐	B ☐	B ☐	B ☐
C ☐	C ☐	C ☐	C ☐	C ☐	C ☐	C ☐	C ☐
D ☐	D ☐	D ☐	D ☐	D ☐	D ☐	D ☐	D ☐
E ☐	E ☐	E ☐	E ☐	E ☐	E ☐	E ☐	E ☐

9	10	11	12	13	14	15	16
A ☐	A ☐	A ☐	A ☐	A ☐	A ☐	A ☐	A ☐
B ☐	B ☐	B ☐	B ☐	B ☐	B ☐	B ☐	B ☐
C ☐	C ☐	C ☐	C ☐	C ☐	C ☐	C ☐	C ☐
D ☐	D ☐	D ☐	D ☐	D ☐	D ☐	D ☐	D ☐
E ☐	E ☐	E ☐	E ☐	E ☐	E ☐	E ☐	E ☐

17	18	19	20	21	22	23	24
A ☐	A ☐	A ☐	A ☐	A ☐	A ☐	A ☐	A ☐
B ☐	B ☐	B ☐	B ☐	B ☐	B ☐	B ☐	B ☐
C ☐	C ☐	C ☐	C ☐	C ☐	C ☐	C ☐	C ☐
D ☐	D ☐	D ☐	D ☐	D ☐	D ☐	D ☐	D ☐
E ☐	E ☐	E ☐	E ☐	E ☐	E ☐	E ☐	E ☐

25	26	27	28	29	30	31	32
A ☐	A ☐	A ☐	A ☐	A ☐	A ☐	A ☐	A ☐
B ☐	B ☐	B ☐	B ☐	B ☐	B ☐	B ☐	B ☐
C ☐	C ☐	C ☐	C ☐	C ☐	C ☐	C ☐	C ☐
D ☐	D ☐	D ☐	D ☐	D ☐	D ☐	D ☐	D ☐
E ☐	E ☐	E ☐	E ☐	E ☐	E ☐	E ☐	E ☐

33	34	35	36	37	38	39	40
A ☐	A ☐	A ☐	A ☐	A ☐	A ☐	A ☐	A ☐
B ☐	B ☐	B ☐	B ☐	B ☐	B ☐	B ☐	B ☐
C ☐	C ☐	C ☐	C ☐	C ☐	C ☐	C ☐	C ☐
D ☐	D ☐	D ☐	D ☐	D ☐	D ☐	D ☐	D ☐
E ☐	E ☐	E ☐	E ☐	E ☐	E ☐	E ☐	E ☐

41 A B C D E

42 A B C D E

43 A B C D E

44 A B C D E

45 A B C D E

46 A B C D E

47 A B C D E

48 A B C D E

49 A B C D E

50 A B C D E

51 A B C D E

52 A B C D E

53 A B C D E

54 A B C D E

55 A B C D E

56 A B C D E

57 A B C D E

58 A B C D E

59 A B C D E

60 A B C D E

61 A B C D E

62 A B C D E

63 A B C D E

64 A B C D E

65 A B C D E

66 A B C D E

67 A B C D E

68 A B C D E

69 A B C D E

70 A B C D E

71 A B C D E

72 A B C D E

BACK

NON VERBAL
TEST 9

MULTIPLE CHOICE

NAME

DATE OF BIRTH

SCORE

1	2	3	4	5	6	7	8
A	A	A	A	A	A	A	A
B	B	B	B	B	B	B	B
C	C	C	C	C	C	C	C
D	D	D	D	D	D	D	D
E	E	E	E	E	E	E	E

9	10	11	12	13	14	15	16
A	A	A	A	A	A	A	A
B	B	B	B	B	B	B	B
C	C	C	C	C	C	C	C
D	D	D	D	D	D	D	D
E	E	E	E	E	E	E	E

17	18	19	20	21	22	23	24
A	A	A	A	A	A	A	A
B	B	B	B	B	B	B	B
C	C	C	C	C	C	C	C
D	D	D	D	D	D	D	D
E	E	E	E	E	E	E	E

25	26	27	28	29	30	31	32
A	A	A	A	A	A	A	A
B	B	B	B	B	B	B	B
C	C	C	C	C	C	C	C
D	D	D	D	D	D	D	D
E	E	E	E	E	E	E	E

33	34	35	36	37	38	39	40
A	A	A	A	A	A	A	A
B	B	B	B	B	B	B	B
C	C	C	C	C	C	C	C
D	D	D	D	D	D	D	D
E	E	E	E	E	E	E	E

NON VERBAL
TEST 9

ANSWERS

Question	1	2	3	4	5	6	7	8
Answer	D	C	D	B	D	E	C	A

Question	9	10	11	12	13	14	15	16
Answer	D	C	C	D	B	D	A	C

Question	17	18	19	20	21	22	23	24
Answer	C	C	D	B	C	A	A	C

Question	25	26	27	28	29	30	31	32
Answer	C	B	B	B	D	C	D	D

Question	33	34	35	36	37	38	39	40
Answer	C	C	D	A	B	B	A	C

Question	A	B	C	D	E
41		■			
42			■		
43				■	
44					■
45					■
46					■
47			■		
48	■				
49	■				
50			■		
51	■				
52		■			
53				■	
54			■		
55		■			
56				■	
57			■		
58		■			
59				■	
60					■
61				■	
62			■		
63			■		
64	■				
65				■	
66			■		
67			■		
68				■	
69		■			
70			■		
71					■
72			■		

Test Teach

BACK

NON VERBAL
TEST 10

ANSWERS

Question	Answer
1	B
2	E
3	D
4	C
5	B
6	E
7	C
8	C
9	C
10	E
11	C
12	C
13	D
14	E
15	D
16	E
17	C
18	B
19	A
20	A
21	C
22	D
23	E
24	A
25	A
26	E
27	E
28	D
29	E
30	B
31	C
32	D
33	E
34	D
35	A
36	D
37	D
38	B
39	B
40	A

Question	A	B	C	D	E
41	□	■	□	□	□
42	□	■	□	□	□
43	□	□	□	■	□
44	□	□	□	□	■
45	■	□	□	□	□
46	□	□	□	■	□
47	□	□	■	□	□
48	□	□	□	■	□
49	□	□	□	□	■
50	■	□	□	□	□
51	□	□	□	■	□
52	□	□	□	□	■
53	□	■	□	□	□
54	□	□	□	■	□
55	□	□	■	□	□
56	■	□	□	□	□
57	□	□	■	□	□
58	□	□	□	■	□
59	□	□	□	■	□
60	□	□	■	□	□
61	□	□	□	□	■
62	□	□	□	■	□
63	□	□	□	■	□
64	□	■	□	□	□
65	□	■	□	□	□
66	□	□	□	□	■
67	□	■	□	□	□
68	■	□	□	□	□
69	■	□	□	□	□
70	□	■	□	□	□
71	□	■	□	□	□
72	□	□	■	□	□

Test Teach

NON VERBAL TEST 11

Question	Answer
1	C
2	C
3	C
4	B
5	D
6	B
7	D
8	E
9	D
10	C
11	B
12	E
13	C
14	E
15	C
16	E
17	B
18	C
19	B
20	A
21	E
22	D
23	A
24	E
25	E
26	B
27	C
28	B
29	A
30	A
31	A
32	C
33	C
34	B
35	A
36	A
37	A
38	D
39	E
40	B

Question	A	B	C	D	E
41	□	□	□	□	■
42	□	□	□	■	□
43	□	■	□	□	□
44	□	□	□	■	□
45	□	□	■	□	□
46	□	□	□	■	□
47	□	□	□	■	□
48	□	□	■	□	□
49	□	■	□	□	□
50	□	□	■	□	□
51	□	□	■	□	□
52	□	□	■	□	□
53	□	□	□	□	■
54	□	□	■	□	□
55	□	□	■	□	□
56	□	■	□	□	□
57	■	□	□	□	□
58	□	□	□	□	■
59	□	□	□	□	■
60	■	□	□	□	□
61	□	□	■	□	□
62	□	□	■	□	□
63	■	□	□	□	□
64	□	□	■	□	□
65	□	□	■	□	□
66	□	□	□	□	■
67	□	■	□	□	□
68	□	□	■	□	□
69	□	□	□	■	□
70	□	□	□	■	□
71	□	□	□	■	□
72	□	■	□	□	□

Test Teach

BACK

NON VERBAL TEST 12

ANSWERS

Question	Answer
1	A
2	D
3	B
4	A
5	E
6	C
7	D
8	B
9	A
10	A
11	D
12	B
13	C
14	B
15	C
16	B
17	A
18	E
19	D
20	C
21	E
22	C
23	D
24	C
25	E
26	D
27	B
28	B
29	C
30	E
31	D
32	E
33	E
34	B
35	B
36	E
37	B
38	A
39	A
40	C

	A	B	C	D	E
41	□	□	□	□	■
42	■	□	□	□	□
43	■	□	□	□	□
44	□	■	□	□	□
45	□	□	■	□	□
46	□	□	■	□	□
47	□	□	■	□	□
48	□	□	□	□	■
49	□	■	□	□	□
50	■	□	□	□	□
51	■	□	□	□	□
52	□	□	□	□	■
53	□	□	□	□	■
54	□	□	□	■	□
55	□	□	■	□	□
56	□	□	■	□	□
57	■	□	□	□	□
58	□	■	□	□	□
59	□	□	□	□	■
60	□	□	□	■	□
61	□	□	□	□	■
62	■	□	□	□	□
63	■	□	□	□	□
64	□	■	□	□	□
65	□	□	■	□	□
66	□	□	□	□	■
67	□	□	■	□	□
68	□	□	□	□	■
69	□	□	□	■	□
70	□	□	□	■	□
71	□	□	■	□	□
72	□	□	□	■	□

Test Teach